Treacherous TRAITORS

PROFILES

Amazing Archaeologists and Their Finds
America's Most Influential First Ladies
America's Third-Party Presidential Candidates
Black Abolitionists and Freedom Fighters
Black Civil Rights Champions
Charismatic Cult Leaders
Courageous Crimefighters
Great Auto Makers and Their Cars
Great Justices of the Supreme Court
Hatemongers and Demagogues
Hoaxers and Hustlers
International Terrorists
Philanthropists and Their Legacies
Soviet Leaders from Lenin to Gorbachev
Top Entrepreneurs and Their Businesses
Top Lawyers and Their Famous Cases
Treacherous Traitors
Women Business Leaders
Women Chosen for Public Office
Women Inventors and Their Discoveries
Women of the U.S. Congress
Women Who Reformed Politics
The World's Greatest Explorers

Treacherous TRAITORS

Nathan Aaseng

The Oliver Press, Inc.
Minneapolis

The Oliver Press, Inc.
Charlotte Square
5707 West 36th Street
Minneapolis, MN 55416-2510

Library of Congress Cataloging-in-Publication Data

Aaseng, Nathan.
Treacherous Traitors / Nathan Aaseng.
p.   cm.—(Profiles)
Includes bibliographical references and index.
    Summary: Profiles ten figures in American history who have
been accused of betraying their country, including Benedict
Arnold, Julius and Ethel Rosenberg, and Aldrich Ames.
ISBN 1-881508-38-2 (lib. bdg.)
1. Traitors—United States—Biography—Juvenile literature.   2.
Treason—United States—History—Juvenile literature. 3. United
States—Politics and government—Juvenile literature [1. Traitors.
2. Treason—History. 3. United States—Politics and
government.] I. Title. II. Series: Profiles (Minneapolis, Minn.)
E183.A2   1997
364.1'31'092273—dc21
[B]   96-29861
                                                                        CIP
                                                                        AC

ISBN: 1-881508-38-2
Profiles XXIII
Printed in the United States of America

03 02 01 00 99 98 97   8 7 6 5 4 3 2 1

Contents

"Treason never prospers," Benjamin Franklin observed in the late 1700s. "If it doth, none dare call it treason." American revolutionaries such as Franklin who became the founding fathers of the United States were "traitors" to the British government that was determined to keep its North American colonies.

Introduction

*T*raitor!

The word is so charged with emotion and dripping with contempt that we can hardly say it without sneering. "I consider your crime worse than murder," declared Judge Irving Kaufman to Julius and Ethel Rosenberg after a jury found the two guilty of betraying their country.

People who know nothing else about Benedict Arnold know him as one of the most treacherous villains in United States history. He secretly sold out his fellow soldiers who had braved death alongside him in their fight for freedom. How could he be anything but completely bankrupt of morals and decency? Americans were so disgusted by what Arnold had done that they left his name off every Revolutionary War memorial. The people of his hometown even tore up the gravestones of family members who shared Benedict Arnold's name.

Judge Irving Kaufman sentenced Julius and Ethel Rosenberg to death for passing information about the atomic bomb to the Soviets.

The nature of treason, however, is often complicated. It is not always easy to say which actions should be considered treasonous. John Brown was condemned to die as a traitor for attacking a federal armory in Virginia. Yet Robert E. Lee, the man who had captured Brown, went on to wage a far more deadly war against the U.S. government. Despite this act, which many would regard as treason, Lee maintains a reputation as one of the most honorable heroes in American history.

In 1945, Germany executed a theologian named Dietrich Bonhoeffer for plotting to overthrow the government of his native land. Bonhoeffer had technically committed treason. But because the government he had tried to topple was the murderous Nazi regime of Adolf Hitler, most people now consider him to have been a hero, not a traitor.

When Daniel Ellsberg leaked to the press secret government documents concerning U.S. involvement in the Vietnam War in the 1970s, many Americans believed he had committed a despicable act of treason. Others claimed, however, that Ellsberg was bravely attempting to steer his country away from a destructive policy.

In basic terms, treason is an attempt to overthrow or damage the lawfully established government of one's native land. Unlike most other crimes, however, treason involves politics. Depending on who remains in power, an act may either be condemned as treasonous or celebrated as heroic.

During a civil war, loyal supporters of the existing government consider themselves to be law-abiding citizens, and they may regard the rebels as traitors. But if the opposition gains power, the tables turn. The rebels then may charge those loyal to the former government with treason for opposing the government that is now in control of the country.

Historically, ruling parties have twisted treason laws to keep themselves in power and protect themselves from criticism. They have considered those who disagreed with them to be traitors. Soviet dictator Josef Stalin, for example, had thousands of "traitors" executed simply because they disagreed with his policies.

Because the founders of the United States were well aware of the potential abuse of treason laws, they made a

Aaron Burr (1756-1836), the third vice-president of the United States, is the highest-ranking American government official to have been tried for treason. Although Burr was found not guilty, most people still considered him a traitor.

special point of creating a very narrow definition of treason in the Constitution:

> Treason against the United States, shall consist only in levying War against them, or in adhering to their Enemies, giving them Aid and Comfort.

Despite this definition, Americans continue to wrestle with the concept of treason. Some of the people in this book, such as Benedict Arnold and John Walker, were caught red-handed betraying their country to its enemies. Others, such as Julius and Ethel Rosenberg and Alger Hiss, protested their innocence to the end. Still others, such as Iva Toguri (known as Tokyo Rose), admitted to certain acts but denied any intention of committing treason.

Even when it is clear that a person has committed a treasonous act, the individual's motives may have been evil or brave and selfless. A greedy man, Aldrich Ames betrayed his fellow agents and caused their deaths so that he could live in luxury. But the morally strict John Brown was stirred by his conscience to sacrifice himself to bring about an end to slavery.

However difficult treachery is to define or to prove, the stories of the people in this book will help to explore the complexity of this crime and the reasons that traitors turn against their native land and their fellow citizens.

Throughout his long career as director of the Federal Bureau of Investigation (FBI), J. Edgar Hoover (1895-1972) zealously upheld the bureau's responsibility to arrest traitors and spies.

Before turning against his fellow Americans, Benedict Arnold (1741-1801) risked his life countless times and suffered a crippling leg injury while fighting the British in the American Revolution.

1

Benedict Arnold
Hero to Villain

*T*he name Benedict Arnold has become a synonym for traitor, but Arnold may have been the greatest general to fight in the American Revolution. He played a key role in more major battles than any other American leader. In fact, the British might well have won the war had Arnold not been on the scene. Almost overnight, however, Benedict Arnold plunged from the heights of heroism to the abyss of shame.

Benedict Arnold was born in Norwich, Connecticut, on January 14, 1741, to one of the most respected families in the American colonies. His great-grandfather had been the first governor of Rhode Island. Arnold's father, also named Benedict, owned a fleet of trading ships.

The elder Benedict, however, squandered his fortune and reputation on alcohol. When the family ran out of money to pay for Benedict's expensive private school in 1754, the 13-year-old had to return home to the embarrassment of living with a drunken father.

Benedict reacted by going to extremes to prove his worth. He was quick to fight anyone who did not show him proper respect. And he was a daredevil who would climb the masts of ships in the harbor and walk on steep roofs of tall buildings whenever he had an audience.

Unable to keep her roaming, hot-tempered son out of trouble, Mrs. Arnold sent him to work for her cousin Daniel Lathrop. The only pharmacy between Boston and New York, Lathrop's booming business had provided him with a mansion surrounded by fabulous gardens. Within five years, Benedict had proved to be so skillful and trustworthy that Lathrop made him his chief clerk at the age of 18. The teenager frequently sailed to Canada, England, and the West Indies to buy and sell supplies.

When Arnold completed his apprenticeship at the age of 21, he set out on his own. With the help of a generous gift from Lathrop, he opened his own shop in New Haven, Connecticut, and sold medicines and books to students at nearby Yale College.

As Arnold's shop prospered, he married and bought three ships to carry imported products from England to the American colonies. He spent much of the next decade at sea, trading goods and amassing a small fortune.

14

Arnold, however, was becoming increasingly angry with the British for hurting his business. In the 1760s, England began to interfere with trade between the colonists and the Caribbean—trade that Arnold depended on. When Americans rebelled against British taxes charged on such items as sugar and rum, Arnold became New Haven's leading smuggler, avoiding taxes by bringing these supplies into the country illegally.

Although he did well in business, Arnold had trouble getting along with people. He drove off his sister's suitor at gunpoint and often challenged people to duels over the slightest disagreements. In the middle of the night, Arnold and his friends would threaten and assault *Tories*—those Americans who supported the British government in its disputes with America.

In the spring of 1775, the quarrels between the American colonies and the British exploded into war. On hearing of the first skirmish at Lexington, Massachusetts, on April 19, 1775, Arnold flew into action. As captain of the local militia, he demanded the key to New Haven's ammunition supply to arm his troops. Because the town had not yet voted to join a war against the British, the authorities refused.

"None but Almighty God shall prevent my marching!" thundered Arnold. The authorities backed down and gave him what he wanted.

On his way to join the battle, Arnold met Colonel Samuel Parsons of the Connecticut militia. Parsons said the Americans at Lexington could not drive out the heavily armed British because the revolutionaries had no cannons. Arnold considered the problem. The British forts along the southern edge of Lake Champlain on the New York frontier were bristling with cannons, he told Parsons—and only a small British force held the forts.

When Arnold reached Boston, he persuaded the Massachusetts authorities to assign him the task of capturing the cannons at Fort Ticonderoga, near Lake Champlain. Now a colonel—with a horse, weapons, and money—Arnold set out to recruit 400 soldiers.

In the meantime, Parsons, recognizing the wisdom of Arnold's plan, proposed to the Connecticut militia that they attack the same fort. Ethan Allen and his Green Mountain Boys, a rough-and-ready collection of Vermont frontiersmen, led the expedition. As Arnold was forming his own unit of men, he learned that Allen's force was already approaching the fort.

Arnold dashed ahead of his army and caught up with Allen on May 8. Colonel Arnold showed the popular commander the Massachusetts orders authorizing him to take charge of capturing Fort Ticonderoga. But the Green Mountain Boys, who made up about half of Allen's force, wanted nothing to do with Arnold. These rugged, independent pioneers had earlier fought under Allen in several skirmishes to protect their land along the New York frontier. They announced they would fight under Allen's command or go home.

Allen compromised and suggested that he and Arnold lead the attack together. The two headstrong leaders must have made a comical sight as they climbed the cliff at the head of the attack force on May 10, each

Ethan Allen had organized the Green Mountain Boys in the early 1770s to prevent their lands in the New Hampshire Grants (now Vermont) from becoming part of New York. They would be just as zealous in defending their rights against Benedict Arnold.

eyeing the other to see that he did not get ahead. Together, they charged through the gates of Fort Ticonderoga. Catching the small British force completely by surprise, the two men and their followers forced a surrender without a fight.

When his men finally arrived at the fort, Arnold sailed north to attack the British naval base at St. Jean on the north end of Lake Champlain. Acting without authorization, Arnold captured four British ships and destroyed five others on May 20. Colonel Arnold had financed much of this expedition with his own money, expecting to be reimbursed by the colonial governments.

These victories at Fort Ticonderoga and St. Jean postponed the threat of British attack from the north for at least a year. But the brash, tactless Arnold had made numerous enemies. Ethan Allen never mentioned Arnold in his official report of the action. And Allen's men warned the revolutionaries' Continental Congress that Arnold was improperly spending the government's money. This was only the first of many times that Arnold would be accused of overspending and even looting to supply himself and his men.

Unfortunately for Arnold, Massachusetts authorities believed his detractors. When a new commander

It took nearly two months for oxen to drag more than 50 cannons on sledges from Fort Ticonderoga, New York, to the American troops stationed in Boston.

arrived at Fort Ticonderoga that summer to relieve
Arnold of his command, the enraged colonel promptly
resigned from the army. On the way home, more bitter
news reached him. His wife, Margaret, had died while he
was away.

Arnold, however, did not sit around and brood.
Shortly after returning home, he heard that Congress
had approved an attack on Canada, which the British controlled. Ever since the fall of Fort Ticonderoga, Arnold
had been urging such a strategy.

Arnold brought an attack plan to the American military commander, George Washington. He proposed
that one group of fighters capture the city of Montreal,
Canada, from the south while another force, led by
Arnold, forge its way through the wilderness to storm
the city of Quebec from the southeast and take control of
the St. Lawrence River. Washington approved the plan.

In mid-September 1775, Colonel Arnold led more
than 1,000 soldiers north into the Maine wilderness. He
estimated that they could reach the St. Lawrence River in
20 days. But the distance from Maine to Quebec was
twice what Arnold had guessed. And the 200 boats he had
ordered for the journey weighed nearly 400 pounds each.
His force had to carry 100 tons of supplies through almost
400 miles of wilderness.

Only half of Arnold's force reached Quebec 51 days
later. He had lost the rest of his troops to death or deser-
tion during the harsh journey as freezing storms had
destroyed their supplies and most of the gunpowder.
Badly outnumbered and short on ammunition, Arnold

had to wait for reinforcements from the American force that by then had captured Montreal.

On New Year's Eve, Arnold attacked during a raging blizzard. His troops fought valiantly in the city's streets, but the offensive failed as the British troops killed or

Arnold's troops nearly starved to death on their way to Quebec. Then they had to wait in the cold Canadian winter for almost two months until the Americans had a large enough force to mount an assault on the British entrenched in the city.

wounded 80 Americans and forced 426 of Arnold's men to surrender. The British, meanwhile, lost only 18 men.

Still vowing to fight on, Arnold limped off the street with a bullet wound in his leg. "I have no thoughts of leaving this proud town until I first enter it in triumph," he wrote to his sister. But when 10,000 British soldiers docked at Quebec in May 1776, Arnold's small force had to flee. Arnold, recently promoted to general, barely caught the last boat to escape the pursuing British.

Not only did the attempt to conquer Canada fail, but the overbearing Arnold continued to make enemies. Ethan Allen's Green Mountain Boys charged him with looting. "Money is this man's god," fumed one, "and to get enough of it he would sacrifice his country."

But Arnold had no time for responding to the charges. The British were launching a campaign that could destroy the American forces. In July 1776, the British moved south from Canada and assembled a powerful fleet on the north shore of Lake Champlain. Arnold realized that with these ships and with the 10,000 soldiers commanded by General Guy Carleton and General John Burgoyne, the British could sail across the lake and down the Hudson River. Eventually, they would link up with General William Howe's huge British force advancing from New York City. This move would cut the colonies in two and give the British complete control over the continent of North America.

Refusing to let that happen, Benedict Arnold hatched a bold plan to build the first American navy on the south end of Lake Champlain. Going over the head

On July 4, 1776, only three days before Arnold introduced his plan for an American navy, the Continental Congress approved the Declaration of Independence. Now the American leaders had become traitors to Great Britain in word as well as in deed.

of General Horatio Gates, his commanding officer, Arnold brought in hundreds of carpenters and sailors to build the necessary ships.

When the British sailed that autumn, the Americans were ready to stop them. Although overmatched, Arnold's fleet slugged it out with the British in a seven-hour battle. As evening fell, the British trapped the remaining American ships, expecting to finish them off in the morning. But under cover of the dark, Arnold slipped his ships, one at a time, past the unsuspecting British fleet. By morning, all the American sailing vessels were gone.

Benedict Arnold in a 1776 engraving by British artist Charles Hart

The British eventually caught up to the fleeing Americans on the lake and fought another fierce battle. But once again, Arnold and his men escaped and made it to shore. Carrying their wounded in their sails, they marched 20 miles through the forest to Fort Ticonderoga to escape the British fleet.

The tiny navy was destroyed, but Arnold's action may have saved his country by slowing down the British advance. Fearful of being caught out in the wilderness during the winter, the British returned to their base in Canada instead of advancing to New York.

Because he did not have to divide his forces to counter the British attack from the north, General Washington's ragged troops were able to survive against a superior British army for another season. Thus, Arnold bought a crucial year's time for the American forces. As naval historian Alfred Thayer Mahan observed, "The little American navy was wiped out, but never had any force, big, or small, lived to a better purpose."

Many Americans, including George Washington, declared Arnold a hero. But Congress passed over Arnold and instead promoted five junior officers to the rank of major general in February 1777. Furious, Arnold again resigned from the army.

When a British force landed in his native Connecticut, however, Arnold jumped back into the fray. With only 400 men at his command, Arnold could not hope to defeat more than 2,000 British soldiers. Arnold was thrown from his wounded horse as his troops were retreating. The British nearly captured him, but Arnold shot his way out of trouble. Although he could not stop the British, his courage won him many admirers.

On May 2, 1777, the colonial government followed Washington's recommendation and finally promoted Arnold to the rank of major general. He returned to the New York frontier where British general John Burgoyne was making another attempt to link up with General Howe. After losing 1,000 men at Bennington in upstate New York, Burgoyne advanced to nearby Saratoga, where he began to face a shortage of supplies.

Burgoyne had to break through the American lines and reach Howe before his food ran out. Sensing the enemy's desperation, Arnold led a crucial charge that drove back the British in the Battle of Saratoga. He also commanded a force that drove off reinforcements trying to reach Burgoyne. Trapped by the American forces and out of food, Burgoyne surrendered his army of nearly 6,000 soldiers to General Gates.

The victory at Saratoga reversed a string of defeats for the Americans and boosted their morale. But again, the taste of victory was bitter for Arnold. In his official report, General Gates—who had not authorized these missions—did not even mention Arnold's contribution. Even worse, Arnold had received a crippling wound in his thigh. "I wish it had been my heart," he said when he realized his leg injury would end his military career.

George Washington, however, learned of Arnold's part in the victory at Saratoga. Wanting to reward Arnold but realizing that the man was too badly hurt to take part in battle, Washington appointed him to the position of

The American victory at Saratoga was a turning point in the Revolutionary War. In the above painting, General John Burgoyne hands over his sword to General Horatio Gates.

military governor of Philadelphia. (American forces had recently recaptured this important colonial city, which earlier had been a Tory stronghold.)

The appointment turned out to be an unfortunate one. Arnold liked to live luxuriously. Believing his country owed him for his sacrifices and brilliant service—as well as for the money he had spent from his own pockets for his armies—he repeatedly spent government funds without accounting for them. People began to question Arnold's loyalty to the American cause and accused him of making illegal purchases, granting special favors to friends, and using his position for his own gain.

Arnold was also too arrogant and stubborn to get along with the citizens of Philadelphia. Worse, he began courting Peggy Shippen, the daughter of a British sympathizer. This was a disastrous move for a public official.

When the Pennsylvania authorities brought eight charges of abuses of military and civil power against him in February 1779, Arnold was livid. "I daily discover so much baseness and ingratitude among mankind that I almost blush at being of the same species," he wrote to his fiancée. He began to hate the colonial government even more than he had hated the British. In May, he secretly sent word to the British that he was considering changing sides. Soon he was negotiating payment with General Henry Clinton, the British commander in chief.

Arnold's civil case came to trial in December 1779. A court-martial found him guilty of only two minor charges—granting an illegal pass to a cargo vessel and misappropriating public wagons. Washington's punishment was merely a mild reprimand, but it stung. Then in April 1780, Congress informed Arnold that he would not be reimbursed for many of the bills—amounting to £3,000 (about $150,000 in today's money)—that he had submitted for purchases on the Quebec expedition.

Arnold, who had never been paid for his military service, grew even more bitter and desperate. He wanted the war to end so he could return to business and earn some money. Arnold also knew that the American government had no money to pay its soldiers, so he became convinced that he would do everyone a favor by finding a way to end the war.

Arnold believed that handing over control of the Hudson River to the British would give them victory. Turning down Washington's generous offer to take charge of the left wing of his army, Arnold instead asked for command of West Point, the cluster of American forts that guarded the Hudson River. After Arnold had been assigned to West Point, he alerted the British that he was willing to turn over the forts for a price. (Ironically, one of the forts had been named Fort Arnold in his honor.)

Late in September 1780, Major John André left the British ship *Vulture*, which was anchored in the Hudson River south of West Point, to meet secretly with Arnold. According to the customs of war, a soldier could be hanged as a spy if he went behind enemy lines, wore a disguise, or carried documents proving his espionage. Major André broke all three rules. When gunfire chased the *Vulture* downstream, André had to ride south through the American lines to get back to territory controlled by his British compatriots. He was disguised as an American and in one boot carried five documents detailing the plans for turning over West Point. But André expected no trouble because he was also carrying written orders from Arnold allowing him to pass the American sentries.

As André approached a British outpost near Tarrytown, New York, three men stopped him. Believing the men to be British or their allies, André identified himself as a British officer. Unfortunately for him, the men were Americans intent on robbing Tories. When they found the documents in André's boot, the three patriots turned him over to the American army.

Despite being a spy, the personable Major John André would charm the American officials who held him prisoner. They regarded André as a gentleman and regretted that they had to punish him for his espionage.

Planning for just such an emergency, Arnold had ordered Colonel John Jameson to inform him if a John Anderson (the name André was using) showed up in the area. Jameson dutifully sent word to Arnold that he had such a man under arrest, but he sent the suspicious documents from André's boot to General Washington, who happened to be visiting West Point.

Arnold received his message as he sat down to eat breakfast with Washington's aides, just before the incriminating documents reached Washington. Realizing his danger, the former patriot excused himself from the table. He galloped to the Hudson and then rowed 18 miles to the *Vulture*, where he found safety with his new allies.

While Arnold was making his escape, Washington received the evidence of his trusted general's treason. The news devastated him, for he had always been Arnold's most faithful supporter. "Arnold has betrayed me," Washington lamented. "Whom can we trust now?"

The immensely popular and respected General George Washington (1732-1799) would be elected the new nation's first president in 1789.

The Americans hanged Major André as a spy, but the man they really wanted to see swing from a tree was Arnold! American soldiers made models of his head as targets for practice shooting. Arnold's treason actually strengthened the American cause since outrage over his betrayal brought Americans together in a greater determination to win the war.

For his treason, Benedict Arnold had requested £20,000 (about $1 million in today's money). This sum would compensate him for the money Congress owed him, other debts he would be unable to collect, and the value of his property. He received less than £6,000.

Arnold further tarnished his reputation in the colonies when he led colonial troops loyal to the British in murderous destruction. In January 1781, he commanded a raid against Richmond, Virginia, in which his forces looted and burned the city and captured more than 30 merchant ships. Seven months later, he organized a raid on New London, Connecticut, only 12 miles from his former home in Norwich. During fierce fighting, Arnold's men set fire to warehouses and shops. Wind spread the fire, destroying 200 homes. Furthermore, his troops slaughtered soldiers at an American garrison even after their leader had surrendered. The episode confirmed the opinion of many Americans that Arnold was the most evil person on the face of the earth.

Arnold's new allies had little more respect for him than the Americans did. Many British did not trust a leader who had sold out the men who had fought alongside him. Unable to muster enough American deserters to complete his regiment, Arnold engaged in no more battles that year. Because they had lost so many men in Arnold's two raids, the British were not disappointed.

Arnold was never to see military action again. Late in 1781, General Charles Cornwallis surrendered a large British army along the coast of Virginia. Arnold was stunned. Sailing to England, he tried to convince the British government that it could still win the war, but Parliament voted to abandon the fight. Arnold's treason had backfired and left him an exile from his homeland.

Benedict Arnold never returned to the United States. After living in England for a time, he set up a trading business in a community of American Tories who had moved to New Brunswick, Canada. But even there his treason had disgraced him. After neighbors burned a dummy labeled "traitor" in front of his home, Arnold and his family returned to England in 1792.

Unable to make as much money as he wanted, Arnold returned to the enterprise at which he had excelled—war. In 1793, he served as a secret agent for the British against their French enemies in the West Indies. The French captured him and planned to do what most Americans had long wished to do—hang him. But the 52-year-old Arnold proved to be as slippery as ever. In the cabin on the ship in which he was held prisoner, he pried up the floorboards to build a raft. During the night, he paddled with his hands to freedom.

Arnold made one last effort to win a fortune. In 1801, he invested in a *privateer*, a privately owned ship that attempts to plunder enemy cargo ships. But the effort failed, and Benedict Arnold the pirate lost most of the money he had put into the project.

Although Arnold received only a fraction of the payment he had requested for his treason, he made more money from the war than any other American general. Profiting from his act of betrayal apparently did not bother him. "I have ever acted from a principle of love to my country," he wrote to George Washington. He even wrote to Congress demanding that it pay him the rest of the officer's salary the American government owed him!

Benedict Arnold died in England on June 14, 1801, unhappy and deeply in debt. To the end, he saw himself as an unappreciated hero. History would remember him not as the "bravest of the brave," as Washington once called him, but as one of the highest ranking officers ever to sell out his country.

Loved and feared in his own time, John Brown (1800-1859) would continue to inspire other militants—including twentieth-century black nationalist Malcolm X—long after his death.

2

John Brown
Lighting the Civil War Fuse

*F*ew people associate John Brown's name with treason. While he conjures up many images—from hero and saint to insane, murdering fanatic—John Brown has little in common with the other people in this book.

Brown was, in fact, the patriotic grandson of a man who died in the American Revolution. Unlike many traitors, Brown was never tempted to sacrifice his principles for money, even though he was in debt much of his life. And he never conspired with any foreign powers against the United States. Yet Brown is one of the few Americans ever executed by the U.S. government for treason.

John Brown was born in Torrington, Connecticut, on May 9, 1800. His parents, Owen and Ruth Brown, were poor farmers. Hoping to build a better life, they moved to farmland in northeastern Ohio in 1805. Ruth died there in 1808, leaving Owen with six small children.

An intensely religious man, Owen Brown raised his children to follow biblical teachings and to value the state of their eternal souls over anything in the world. He strongly believed that God created all people equal, and, unlike most other white people of his time, he maintained that black people should have equal rights under the law. Slavery, he believed, was a terrible stain on the honor of

Owen Brown left his church and resigned his Ohio government post when some of his colleagues endorsed sending blacks to Africa instead of letting them live as free American citizens.

the United States. A leader in the antislavery movement in Ohio, Brown sheltered runaway slaves in his home when they fled the South and sought freedom in Canada.

Young John Brown, a reserved and serious boy, absorbed his father's strong religious convictions and dreamed of attending a seminary to become a minister. But eye trouble prevented him from reading as much as he needed to, so he had to give up on the ministry.

Instead, John returned to the farm work he knew. He worked well with animals and showed responsibility beyond his years. At the age of 16, John was a supervisor at his father's leather-tanning factory.

John Brown built his own log cabin a mile from his father's house and began farming on his own while still a teenager. At the age of 20, he married Dianthe Lusk, the sister of a friend. In 1825, they moved to rural western Pennsylvania, where Brown worked tirelessly to run a large farm and a prosperous tannery. His operations were successful and he became a leading member of the rural community.

Success did not change Brown's convictions. Each morning, he led his employees and family in a prayer service before work began. Although a strict parent, he was generous to neighbors and to strangers.

The 1830s were a struggle for Brown. In 1832, Dianthe died in childbirth. Like his own father, Brown found himself alone with 5 small children. The following year, he married Mary Ann Day. Then in 1835, John and his wife and children moved back to Ohio. The couple had 13 more children. Brown's attempts to provide for this growing family suffered a blow when an economic depression reduced the value of his land to almost nothing. He fell deeply into debt.

Then John Brown found a mission. In 1837, a mob in Alton, Illinois, killed Elijah Lovejoy, a Presbyterian minister whose antislavery newspaper had enraged southerners and southern sympathizers. At a meeting called to protest the murder, Brown was moved to change the course of his life. "Here, before God in the presence of these witnesses," he announced solemnly, "I consecrate my life to the destruction of slavery."

After three of his printing presses had been destroyed by proslavery mobs, Elijah Lovejoy swore he would defend his newspaper. On November 7, 1837, Lovejoy was murdered by marauding townspeople intent on shutting down his antislavery publication.

For many years, Brown was in no position to carry out that vow. He lost almost everything he owned to creditors and finally went bankrupt in 1842. The following year, he suffered through the deaths of four of his children from dysentery, an infectious disease.

The heartbroken Brown worked tirelessly to get back on his feet. His next venture—an attempt to form a wool cooperative that would give growers control over the prices they received for their product—also failed. But his fight against the powerful wool manufacturers showed both his idealism and his inability to change his plans to achieve success. These characteristics would play a large role in his later activities as a militant abolitionist.

During his years in the wool business, Brown began to think more and more about the slavery issue. Eager to make contact with other abolitionists, in 1849 he moved his family to North Elba, New York, a community of free blacks established by prominent antislavery activist Gerrit Smith. There he befriended his black neighbors while building schools and doing farm work.

The next year, Congress passed the Fugitive Slave Act, a law that made the federal government responsible for catching runaway slaves. Helping slaves escape was now a federal crime. Furthermore, federal marshals could force local citizens to help them track down runaways. Refusing to obey a law that violated his religious beliefs, Brown organized such fierce opposition among the black citizens of North Elba and Springfield, Massachusetts (where his wool operation had been based), that slave catchers avoided those areas.

In the next several years, Brown had to travel almost nonstop between his beloved new home in North Elba; Springfield, where he was defending himself from lawsuits filed by wool growers over his business failure; and the state of Ohio, where he and his sons still raised sheep for wool. Then national events changed his life again. In May 1854, Congress passed the Kansas-Nebraska Act over fierce antislavery opposition. The act gave to the citizens of the two new states *popular sovereignty*—the right to vote on whether to allow slavery in their state.

Everyone assumed Nebraska would enter the union as a free state, but the territory of Kansas might go either way. Immediately, both those who favored and those who opposed slavery began recruiting people to settle in Kansas. Five of these antislavery settlers were John Brown's sons. The young men arrived in Kansas in the spring of 1855, attracted by the promise of good farmland and a chance to strike a blow against slavery.

The fight between proslavery and antislavery forces in Kansas grew savage. Proslavery leaders swore to angry crowds of slaveholders that they would murder antislavery settlers. The outgunned "free-state" men were fighting for their lives. Brown's oldest son, John Jr., sent his father a letter to ask him to send knives, pistols, and rifles. "We need them more than we do bread," he wrote.

Determined to fight once again, Brown left his wife and younger children in the summer of 1855 and arrived in Kansas in October with the weapons. Brown's son John Jr. was a leader of the antislavery forces. Convinced that the state election held in March had been a fraud, the

John Brown had this picture taken the year he went to Kansas to help his sons fight the proslavery settlers.

antislavery group had met in August to write their own free-state constitution and plan the election of free-state legislators. John Brown Jr. was elected to this legislature in January 1856, but President Franklin J. Pierce sent in federal troops to support the proslavery government and disband the "rebellion."

Free-state men were under siege, and John Brown and his sons became increasingly convinced that only violence would settle the slavery question in Kansas. A few proslavery and antislavery men had been attacked or killed in the past months, and, in December 1855, war almost broke out as a wild proslavery militia—the Missouri Border Ruffians—threatened to storm Lawrence, Kansas, a town dominated by free-staters. Determined to stand up for his beliefs in the face of violence, in April 1856 John Brown Jr. formed the Pottawatomie Rifles militia group to defend antislavery settlers.

The following month, Lawrence was again attacked by Missouri invaders. While John Jr. commanded the Rifles, John Brown led his other sons to Lawrence to fight the invaders. Before the defenders arrived, however, they met a messenger on the road who told them the people in the frontier town had given up without a fight.

The slaveholders seemed to be winning everywhere. As the Browns were absorbing the news that the Border Ruffians were looting Lawrence, they learned that anti-slavery senator Charles Sumner of Massachusetts had been brutally beaten by South Carolina congressman Preston Brooks on the floor of the U.S. Senate.

In a murderous rage, Brown decided to strike hard against slavery. Late on the night of May 24, 1856, he and several of his followers—including his sons Owen, Salmon, Oliver, and Frederick, and son-in-law Henry Thompson—knocked on the door of a proslavery family near Pottawatomie, Kansas. They dragged a father and his two grown sons outside and hacked them to death. The group then killed two more proslavery men on nearby farms. Brown never confessed to these acts, and few people outside of Kansas knew of this stain on his character until well after his death.

As something like civil war raged in Kansas, Brown became a fugitive from justice, hiding in the woods to elude proslavery trackers. On June 2, 1856, Brown led the

The speech by Charles Sumner (pictured here) that enraged Preston Brooks was "The Crime against Kansas." In his speech, Sumner attacked the views of South Carolina senator Andrew Pickens Butler, who was Brooks's uncle.

free-state forces to victory in the Battle of Black Jack, which did much for the spirits of the antislavery movement and for John Brown's reputation as a fierce fighter for the cause. But "Bleeding Kansas," as this period is called, took its toll on the Brown family. Their settlement, Brown's Station, was destroyed, and the women and children of the family had to flee for their safety. In response to the Pottawatomie massacre, proslavery men beat and imprisoned John Jr. and his brother Jason, even though neither of them had taken part in the killings. They also murdered Frederick Brown when they caught him in August.

After hiding out for months, John Brown left Kansas in October 1856. He planned to raise money in the East to buy weapons to defend Kansas against the raiders from Missouri. But by the time he had purchased 200 rifles for the free-state men, the antislavery forces no longer needed his help. A new governor who upheld legitimate elections had been appointed, and people opposing slavery easily won the legislature in October 1857. Kansas was now a free state. When Brown returned, he found the proslavery forces had quieted down.

Despite the victory of the antislavery activists at the ballot box in Kansas, Brown believed that southerners would give up slavery only if forced to do so. He even predicted that if the antislavery Republicans won the next presidential election, the South would withdraw from the Union. "We have reached a point where nothing but war can settle the question," Brown warned. "The crimes of this guilty . . . land . . . will never be purged away . . . but with Blood." Brown decided to take bold action to wake up the complacent people of the North so they would be ready for the great battle to free the slaves.

The more he thought, the grander Brown's ideas became. He proposed to start a large-scale rebellion, believing his army might seize enough land to create an interracial state somewhere in the South. Brown planned to capture enough weapons and ammunition to arm a guerrilla army. Then, from bases in the Appalachian Mountains, soldiers would sweep down and lead slaves into their mountain camps. Eventually, the gathered forces would launch a revolution against the slaveholding South.

Although a successful rebellion against the federal government and the southern slaveholders seemed highly unlikely, Brown won the financial support of six prominent abolitionists in March 1858. He planned to recruit northern blacks for his small invading army and he believed that slaves would rally to his call in such numbers that he would command a powerful force. In May 1858, Brown met with a group of free blacks in Canada to write a constitution and elect government officials for the state he planned to create following the rebellion.

Brown had discussed his plan to free the slaves with the famous abolitionist Frederick Douglass (1818-1895), whom Brown had first met in 1847. He hoped that Douglass would help him recruit northern blacks and then lead the new state they would form after the rebellion.

The attack was originally scheduled for the summer of 1858, but it was delayed because of concern that the government suspected a plot. Later that year, however, Brown led an excursion that made him believe he could expect massive public support for his planned insurrection. In December 1858, Brown fulfilled a life's dream by liberating 11 slaves in Missouri and leading them to freedom with the help of many antislavery activists who risked their lives by sheltering Brown and his group on their way to Canada. Abolitionists celebrated Brown's action in speeches and articles.

As the first site of his attack on slavery, Brown chose the federal arsenal at Harpers Ferry, Virginia, where

John Brown in the late 1850s. After the conflicts in Kansas, Brown became increasingly militant in his plans to end slavery.

weapons and ammunition were manufactured and stored. In July 1859, he rented a farm in Maryland, seven miles from Harpers Ferry, and sent for his daughter and daughter-in-law to give neighbors the impression that this was a family farm and not the headquarters of a revolutionary group. Then Brown laid plans for the attack.

On the night of October 16, 1859, Brown and his 21-man army, including 3 of his sons, set out to capture Harpers Ferry. They could hardly have chosen a more difficult target, for the town was tucked between two rivers and the mountains. Even if Brown could get into the town, his enemies would be able to trap him simply by seizing the two bridges. Brown further invited disaster once he entered Harpers Ferry by dividing his force into small groups, none of which was strong enough to hold off more than a handful of people.

The raid began quietly as two men rode ahead of the group, crossed a bridge, and captured the town's night watchman. Brown left guards on the bridge while other members of his band raided the weapons factories. Brown's group captured the armory guards and about 30 townspeople and held them as hostages in a firehouse. Ironically, the first man that Brown's antislavery liberators killed was a black baggage attendant at the train station who had walked over the bridge to see what was going on.

Although Brown's men had cut the telegraph lines from the town, church bells signaled the alarm to neighboring villages. Late that night, a train pulled into town. Most commanders would have kept the train under guard to keep word of the raid from reaching help, but Brown let the train proceed to spread the news of his seizure of Harpers Ferry.

Brown's invasion plan quickly crumbled. Angry citizens grabbed their weapons and rushed to defend their town. They recaptured the two bridges so quickly that Brown's rear guard never even made it into Harpers Ferry.

Brown might have escaped had he not chosen to wait for the slaves and antislavery whites to flock to his side. He thought he could trade his hostages for safe passage even if he was completely surrounded. But help never came.

The townsfolk and the local militia cut off and killed small pockets of the raiders who were hiding in the town. They trapped most of Brown's remaining men in the firehouse. When Brown sent out two men under a flag of truce in an attempt to make a deal that would allow them to escape, the militia shot them both.

Meanwhile, news of the attack reached Washington. Secretary of War John B. Floyd sent Colonel Robert E. Lee to the scene with marines from the Washington Naval Yard. When Lee and his troops arrived at Harpers Ferry on the following night, Brown and six of his men were barricaded in the firehouse with their hostages.

The next morning, Lee ordered Brown to surrender immediately. When Brown refused, Lieutenant J. E. B. Stuart led the assault. Using a ladder as a battering ram, the marines broke down one of the doors. The final fight lasted only a few minutes. Slashed by swords and severely beaten, John Brown was arrested. Two of his sons died in the Harpers Ferry fiasco.

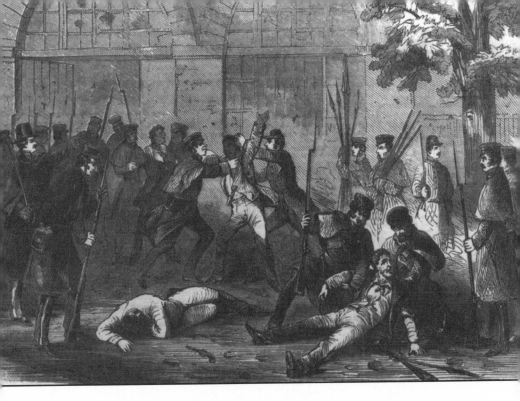

U.S. marines subdued Brown and his men outside the Harpers Ferry firehouse. Not one slave had willingly joined the short-lived rebellion.

Brown was charged with treason against the state of Virginia. Fearful that enraged townspeople would lynch the militant abolitionist, the state rushed his case to trial.

Desperate to save Brown's life, his family members argued that he was insane. John Brown, however, rejected that defense. Realizing that eloquent words could succeed where bold action had brought only disaster, the would-be revolutionary defended himself and used the trial to decry slavery as a crime against God and humanity. He insisted that his actions in trying to free slaves were justified. And he declared that he would gladly give up his life if that would inspire others to take up the cause of freedom.

On October 31, 1859, only two weeks after Brown's capture, a jury found him guilty of treason, and Judge Richard Parker sentenced him to be hanged. On December 2, 1859, John Brown climbed the scaffold under his own power and went to his death.

John Brown had believed that even if his raid on Harpers Ferry failed, his action might cause a war over slavery. In hanging, Brown accomplished the task he had botched so badly at Harpers Ferry—forcing the American people to take action on slavery. Now the entire nation was talking about John Brown. Southerners viewed him as a traitor and a madman, but many northerners saw him as a martyr and the greatest of patriots.

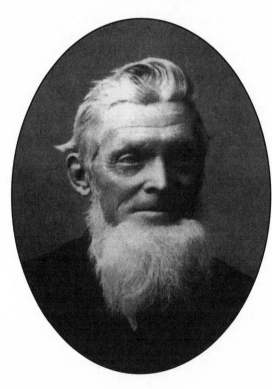

John Brown's son Jason shown as an elderly man. Although Jason had been appalled by the Pottawatomie massacre and had refused to fight at Harpers Ferry, he never lost his admiration for his father.

Robert E. Lee (1807-1870) had defended his government against John Brown. But less than 17 months later, he would command rebel forces against the United States in the Civil War.

Ironically, within two years of Brown's death, those who had brought Brown to justice for treason did exactly what they had hanged Brown for—they took up arms against the U.S. government. Robert E. Lee, J. E. B. Stuart, and Thomas J. Jackson, a soldier who had watched Brown hang, would become three of the most important generals in the Confederate cause. Another young cavalryman at the hanging, John Wilkes Booth, just over five years later would kill the president who freed the slaves.

"John Brown's Body" became a rallying song of the Northern troops as they marched into the Civil War. On January 1, 1863, President Abraham Lincoln took a huge step in fulfilling Brown's dream when he signed the Emancipation Proclamation, which signaled the beginning of the end of slavery in the United States.

*In the 1930s, Alger Hiss (1904-1996) was an
idealistic liberal in President Franklin D. Roosevelt's
New Deal government.*

3

Alger Hiss
Communist Spy in the Government?

*T*he greater a person's influence and power, the greater the possible consequences of his or her treason. That was why Americans found the charges leveled against Alger Hiss in 1948 particularly shocking. Hiss was one of the most highly placed U.S. government officials ever to be publicly accused of betraying his country.

The Hiss case concerns one of the strangest claims of treason in American history. Throughout his long life, Hiss maintained his innocence. And for a person with access to such high levels of government, he caused little if any apparent damage by reportedly passing state secrets to the Soviet Union. Yet Congressman Richard M. Nixon of California, a member of the House Un-American Activities Committee, accused Hiss of being involved in "the most serious series of treasonable activities which has been launched against the government in the history of America."

Furthermore, the U.S. government never actually charged Hiss with treason. His questionable activities did not come to the attention of the public until the *statute of limitations*—the time limit in which authorities must file charges for a crime—had expired. In fact, Hiss never would have spent a day in prison had he not sued the person who accused him of having been a Communist!

Alger Hiss was born on November 11, 1904, in Baltimore, Maryland. When he was only a toddler, his father committed suicide. Despite this tragedy and the lack of a fatherly role model, Hiss was a serious and dedicated student who planned to become a lawyer. He was among the top students in his classes at the highly regarded universities Johns Hopkins and Harvard. After he graduated from Harvard Law School in 1929, he took a job as a law clerk for Oliver Wendell Holmes, the legendary Supreme Court justice.

In 1933, another legal giant, Felix Frankfurter, recruited the promising young lawyer to join the administration of President Franklin D. Roosevelt. Hiss first worked as a lawyer for the Department of Agriculture. He rose quickly through the ranks of government, moving up to important positions in the U.S. Senate, the Department of Justice, the Office of the Solicitor General (the lawyer representing the government in legal cases), and the State Department.

During World War II, Hiss had great influence over American foreign policy. He was one of Roosevelt's advisors at Yalta in 1945 when the U.S. president met with Soviet leader Josef Stalin and British prime minister Winston Churchill to plan postwar policies.

At the end of the war, Hiss served as secretary-general of the international conference that created the

Expecting Germany's surrender, British prime minister Winston Churchill (left), U.S. president Franklin D. Roosevelt (center), and Soviet premier Josef Stalin met at Yalta in the Soviet Union in February 1945. Some of the Yalta agreements were later criticized for allowing the Soviet Union to expand its control of Eastern Europe.

United Nations. According to Hiss, his proudest moment in government was flying home from the United Nations conference in San Francisco to Washington, carrying the charter for the new organization to President Harry S. Truman. The modest Hiss discounted his own importance in the matter by joking that, unlike himself, the charter had a parachute to protect it in case of an accident!

Hiss left government service in 1947 to accept a position as president of the Carnegie Endowment for International Peace. There, out of the public spotlight, he continued to be a capable administrator.

Most Americans never would have heard of Alger Hiss were it not for Whittaker Chambers, an editor for *Time* magazine. Chambers was a brilliant writer—the best the magazine ever had, according to *Time* cofounder and editor-in-chief, Henry Luce. But Chambers harbored a gnawing secret. During the 1930s, he had worked as an underground agent for the Soviet Union.

In 1938, however, Chambers had experienced a change of heart about Communism and began to believe that this political philosophy led to totally evil forms of government. Since then, the writer had often spoken out against Communism, warning of Communist agents in the U.S. government.

Following World War II, as the Soviet Union's goal of spreading Communism began to seem more threatening, Congress became greatly concerned about Communist infiltration of the national government. On August 2, 1948, the House Un-American Activities Committee summoned Chambers to tell what he knew about Communists in the U.S. government. Chambers, who believed his old friends in the party were not bad people, was reluctant to name names. But finally, in a voice so quiet that those present had to strain to hear him, Chambers named eight government officials as members of the Communist Party. Among those were Alger Hiss and his brother Donald Hiss.

Chambers said that Alger Hiss had been a part of a Communist scheme to influence American government policy. When questioned, Hiss indignantly stated, "I am not and never have been a member of the Communist Party." Furthermore, Hiss insisted that he had never met Whittaker Chambers and could not understand why the writer was making up these stories.

Whittaker Chambers spent six years in the Communist underground in the United States and sent information he received from government officials to the Soviet Union.

Hiss (far right) sits next to his lawyer on August 5, 1948, the first day he appeared before the House Un-American Activities Committee. Elizabeth Bentley (left), a former Communist spy, named many people working for the government as Communist agents.

Chambers, however, was able to describe in detail the interior of Hiss's house, and he knew personal information, such as the fact that Mrs. Hiss called her husband "Hilly." He told the committee in closed session that Hiss was an avid bird watcher who was particularly thrilled about having once seen a prothonotary warbler.

In the course of later questioning by the committee, a congressman got Hiss to talk excitedly about having seen just such a warbler. For someone who supposedly had never met Hiss, Chambers obviously knew a great deal about the former government official.

After reading about Chambers's testimony in the newspaper, Hiss changed his story. When he was shown a photograph of Chambers, Hiss said that he could be a freelance writer he had known as George Crosley. Hiss said he had given Crosley a car to use and had rented an apartment to him and his family in 1935.

Under further questioning, however, Hiss wavered between whether he had sold, given, or loaned Crosley the car. The House Un-American Activities Committee grew even more suspicious when Hiss seemed to change his story to fit the latest revealed facts. In addition, the committee found little evidence that anyone else had known a George Crosley.

On August 17, the two men were brought face to face before the committee. Hiss said Chambers was the George Crosley he had known, but he still insisted he had never had anything to do with the Communist Party. Chambers identified Hiss as his closest friend in the Communist Party and claimed he had tried to persuade Hiss to quit the party. As a witness before the committee, Chambers was protected from legal prosecution by the government or by anyone else. Hiss dared Chambers to make the same statements outside the committee room.

Chambers accepted the challenge. On a radio program he said that Hiss had been a Communist and might still be one. In response, on September 27, 1948, Hiss filed a $75,000 slander lawsuit against Chambers, accusing the writer of spreading vicious lies about him.

Hiss hoped the lawsuit would clear his name, but instead it lit the fuse of his own destruction. Chambers's initial charges would not have gotten Hiss into legal trouble because being a Communist was not a crime. But Hiss had forced Chambers to prove his charges by suing him. In November, Chambers revealed much more damaging information about Hiss. He produced copies of confidential State Department documents that he said Hiss had given him in 1938 to pass on to the Soviets.

Hiss now stood accused of treason, and government prosecutors stepped in to bring him to justice. But since the crimes Chambers claimed he had committed had taken place more than 10 years before, the time limit during which the government could prosecute Hiss had run out. The only charges prosecutors could bring against him were two counts of *perjury*, or lying under oath—one count for denying he had given classified government documents to Chambers and the second for lying about his friendship with Chambers.

Hiss's perjury trial, which began on May 31, 1949, basically came down to one man's word against the other's. "If you don't believe Chambers," U.S. attorney Thomas Murphy told the jury, "then we have no case."

Chambers repeated the testimony he had given Congress. He told of his years in the Communist underground and described in detail his friendship with Hiss. Then Chambers produced 4 notes in Hiss's handwriting, 65 typed pages of State Department reports, and 4 rolls of 35-millimeter film showing 58 more pages of State Department documents.

The documents dealt with such issues as the Japanese invasion of China, Nazi Germany's relations with Austria, and trade negotiations with Germany during the late 1930s. The press nicknamed these documents the "Pumpkin Papers" because Chambers had stashed them inside a pumpkin on his Maryland farm.

Chambers claimed that Hiss had brought these classified documents home for his wife to type and had then handed Chambers the copies to deliver to Soviet secret agents. A typewriting expert testified that almost all the papers were typed on an old Woodstock typewriter that the Hisses had used in the 1930s.

Denying everything, Hiss claimed that he had given away the typewriter prior to the time Chambers claimed he had received the documents. To create doubt about Chambers's story, Hiss's lawyers tried to portray the writer as an alcoholic and a compulsive liar who had used 17 different aliases during his lifetime. They pointed out that in the past Chambers had lied about his connections with the Communist Party. He had even changed his story under oath—first denying that Hiss was involved in spying and then accusing him of being a spy. Hiss's lawyers told the jury that Chambers was an unstable character who lived in a fantasy world.

Hiss's defense rested mostly on his respected public record and his credibility as a witness. Well-known government figures such as his former supervisor in the State Department, Assistant Secretary of State Francis Sayre, and Supreme Court Justice Felix Frankfurter stepped forward to speak in support of Hiss's character.

In the end, some jurors believed Alger Hiss while others believed Whittaker Chambers. Because of this, they were a *hung jury* that was unable to reach a verdict during their deliberations. In November 1949, the government retried the case with a new jury.

The retrial repeated most of the information from the previous trial, with a few exceptions. The defense tried a new tack—bringing to the stand a psychologist who diagnosed Chambers as a chronic liar. The government had other witnesses, however, to back up Chambers's credibility. Under oath, a confessed Soviet spy named Hede Massing stated that she had been aware of Hiss's connection with the Communists. In fact, she had once been irritated when she found that she and Hiss were recruiting the same man, Noel Field, for their spy

American diplomat Noel Field and his wife, Herta, shortly before they fled the United States. Field, a Communist agent, soon lost the trust of the Soviets and was imprisoned in one of Stalin's infamous purges in 1949.

ring. The government also called Chambers's former maid, who swore that she had seen Alger Hiss and his wife at her employer's house in the years from 1934 to 1936. Her testimony contradicted Hiss's statements that he had not been a close friend of Chambers.

On January 21, 1950, the jury at his second trial found Hiss guilty on both perjury counts. The jurors concluded that Hiss had given classified government documents to Chambers and had lied about their friendship. Hiss entered federal prison in Lewisburg, Pennsylvania, on March 22, 1951, to begin a five-year sentence.

Any damage that Alger Hiss may have done to the United States has been difficult to determine. The film and documents that Chambers produced as evidence of Hiss's treason contained only a few unspectacular government secrets in a pile of routine information. The Hiss case is noteworthy primarily for the courtroom drama it produced and for its impact on the three principal characters—Alger Hiss, Whittaker Chambers, and Richard Nixon.

Hiss took his punishment with the "gentleness and sweetness of character" that Chambers said had made him so reluctant to testify against his former friend. "Three years in jail is a good corrective to three years at Harvard," Hiss told his son during his sentence. In the course of almost four years in prison, Hiss taught a convict to read and write so that the man could send a letter to his wife for the first time.

Hiss served 44 months of his 60-month sentence before his release in 1954. Afterward, he worked as a salesman, selling stationery. He spent the rest of his life trying to convince people that the charges against him were false.

Hiss's claims received a boost in October 1992. At that time, Russian general Dmitri Volkogonov researched the documents in the Soviet archives for evidence of Hiss's involvement as a Communist spy. He came to the "firm conclusion that Alger Hiss was not ever or anywhere recruited as an agent of the intelligence services of the Soviet Union." Many members of the media accepted this report and proclaimed Hiss innocent of espionage.

A month later, Volkogonov retracted his statement, and research into Hungarian government files supported Chambers's story. The files included statements by Noel Field, a Communist agent who had worked with Hiss at the U.S. State Department, confirming that Hiss had been a fellow spy. Hiss died in 1996 without establishing his innocence.

In the end, Whittaker Chambers may have suffered more from the case than Hiss. The publicity over his work as a Communist spy and the testimony that he had a psychopathic personality ruined his career. *Time* magazine forced Chambers to leave his job as a senior editor, and he would remain an outcast for the rest of his life. Two decades after Chambers's death in 1961, President Ronald Reagan recognized his sacrifice by posthumously awarding him the Medal of Freedom, the highest civilian honor bestowed by the United States.

The man who profited most from the Hiss affair was a young congressman from California who had played

*Congressman Richard M. Nixon reads one of the
thousands of letters he received about the Alger Hiss
case. The public was terrified about the possibility
that there were Communists in the U.S. government.*

a leading role on the House Un-American Activities
Committee during the Hiss hearings. Many observers
praised Representative Richard Nixon for exposing Hiss.
This favorable publicity boosted Nixon into the national
spotlight and set him on the road that eventually led to his
election as president of the United States in 1968.

Mildred Gillars (1900-1988), better known as the hated "Axis Sally," in the custody of U.S. counterintelligence officers in Berlin, Germany, after World War II

4

Axis Sally and Tokyo Rose
Voices of Treason?

*D*uring World War II, American soldiers frequently heard alluring female voices talking to them from enemy headquarters. These radio announcers were part of propaganda programs designed to destroy the morale of American fighting men. In addition to playing soothing music, the women's job was to ridicule the Allied war effort. They attempted to make soldiers homesick and drive them to despair with false information. In Europe, soldiers tuned in to "Axis Sally" (Germany, Italy, and Japan were known as the "Axis" powers), while troops in the Pacific listened to "Tokyo Rose."

These propaganda efforts backfired as American soldiers totally discounted the devious messages wedged in between the musical selections. Ironically, many servicemen looked forward to the programs as a humorous break from the routine of everyday life in the military.

Other Americans were enraged that some of these announcers were American. After the end of the war, the U.S. government brought treason charges against two women identified as Axis Sally and Tokyo Rose. Both were convicted and served time in prison for their crimes.

These two cases had nothing else in common. Although there was no doubt that Axis Sally was a woman named Mildred Gillars, there was no such person as Tokyo Rose. Iva Toguri, whom the U.S. government tried for treason, was a hapless scapegoat convicted for broadcasts made by dozens of women in Japan.

Mildred Sisk was born in Portland, Maine, in 1900. After attending Ohio Wesleyan University for a few years, she left school in 1922 to become an actress. Failing at that, Mildred Gillars, as she was now called, left for Europe in 1929 to be with Max Otto Koischewitz, a native German who had taught at Hunter College in New York City. Koischewitz, a married man, had moved back to Germany to take a position in the government.

Gillars later offered many conflicting accounts of her life in Europe during the 1930s. According to various reports, she studied music and worked as a model in Paris and was a dressmaker in Algeria in northern Africa. She was also a piano student in Dresden, Germany, and an English teacher in Berlin.

When World War II broke out at the end of the decade, Germany's Nazi government recognized women like Gillars as a valuable asset. While its enemies would have no interest in radio programs broadcast in German, they might pay attention to broadcasters who spoke English in a seductive voice. Koischewitz, who was in charge of Radio Berlin's propaganda broadcasts, recruited Gillars to be a disc jockey for one of the shows in 1940.

At the time Gillars began working for Radio Berlin, German crowds were flocking to see Adolf Hitler (center), the dictator who had squelched all political opposition and was already rounding up Jews, Communists, homosexuals, and others in concentration camps.

Gillars found the offer too tempting to resist. Not only was she in love with Koischewitz, but she also had been struggling to earn a living. Radio Berlin offered her a good salary and a chance to become a celebrity. After the United States entered the war, she played popular American music on her "Home, Sweet Home" radio program, which Germany beamed to American soldiers in England and North Africa. In between songs, "Sally," as she called herself, mocked U.S. president Franklin Roosevelt and made such comments as "Damn all the Jews who have made this war possible!"

By early 1944, Germany had firm control of the European continent, but the Nazis feared that the Allies— the Americans and the British—were preparing to invade Europe from England. As part of Germany's propaganda effort, Gillars broadcast a program that Koischewitz wrote called "Vision of an Invasion" on May 11, 1944. In this dramatic story, an actor portraying a soldier from the state of Ohio told of the horrors he experienced while crossing the English Channel to attack German forces occupying France. The American soldiers' screams of agony and sobs of despair were meant to demoralize the troops who would soon be making that crossing.

Less than a month after Radio Berlin aired that broadcast, the Allies did launch an invasion at Normandy, France, on June 6, 1944. Unlike the event depicted in the broadcast, however, the Normandy campaign succeeded, and Germany surrendered within a year on May 7, 1945.

Koischewitz died during the final days of the war. Mildred Gillars wandered, homeless and starving, until a

At dawn on D-Day—June 6, 1944—Allied ships cross the English Channel to land soldiers in France, launching the Normandy invasion.

U.S. counterintelligence officer found her in Berlin later that year. The much-hated celebrity was arrested, but she was later released without being charged with any crime.

Not all Americans, however, were willing to let the matter rest. Pressured by war veterans, the government indicted Gillars on 10 counts of treason and brought her to the United States in August 1948 to stand trial.

The trial of Axis Sally began in Washington, D.C., nearly six months later on January 25, 1949. The U.S. Office of War Information produced a recording of the "Vision of an Invasion" broadcast. Former American prisoners of war (POWs) testified bitterly against Gillars's claim that she simply used her broadcasts to help American prisoners send recorded messages.

According to these witnesses, when Gillars visited POW camps in Germany, France, and Holland during the war, she claimed to represent the Red Cross. She invited the prisoners to record personal messages and promised to send these messages to their loved ones in the United States. Instead, they contended, she used excerpts out of context on her show for propaganda purposes.

Furthermore, one ex-POW said that after he refused to cooperate with Gillars, she told him he would be sorry. Shortly thereafter, the Germans sent him to a concentration camp.

On the stand, Gillars at first denied committing treason. She claimed that she loved the United States and that the Nazis had forced her to take part in the broadcasts at a time when she had no other way to support herself. But on her second day of testimony, Gillars confessed to making the broadcasts to please Koischewitz. She had been his puppet, she said, and had been unable to stand up to him.

After a six-week trial, the jury deliberated for more than 17 hours before finding Gillars guilty of treason on March 10, 1949. The members of the jury did not accept her claim that she had participated in Radio Berlin propaganda broadcasts only because Koischewitz had forced her to do so. One of the most damaging pieces of information against her was that she had received a huge salary for her work—three times the pay of most other German broadcasters at the time.

As punishment for her treason, Mildred Gillars paid a $10,000 fine and served 12 years in a federal prison in

Alderson, West Virginia. When she left prison in 1961, she avoided the public spotlight and found work at a convent school in Columbus, Ohio, where she taught music and German. At the age of 72, she returned to her old school, Ohio Wesleyan, and finally obtained a bachelor's degree. She died on July 25, 1988, at the age of 87.

Tokyo Rose was far more infamous than Axis Sally. Virtually all of the 2 million Americans stationed in the Pacific knew the nickname of the honey-voiced radio temptress who beckoned them from Radio Tokyo. Greetings such as "Good evening again to the forgotten men, the American fighting men" introduced the soldiers to another program of music and light banter.

Most soldiers welcomed the broadcasts as a relief from boredom and stress. They let their imaginations run wild about this mysterious woman whom they only heard but never saw. Stories and rumors spread about the gorgeous seductress, a hypnotic sorceress who taunted and tormented Americans in their own language.

After Japan surrendered on August 14, 1945, American reporters searched the country for Tokyo Rose. Reporter Clark Lee tracked down Iva Toguri, a Japanese-American woman who was working as a broadcaster for Radio Tokyo. Confessing she was Tokyo Rose, Toguri set off an avalanche of publicity about the notorious traitor.

Iva Toguri was born, ironically, on the most patriotic of American holidays—the Fourth of July—in 1916. She was the first member of her family to hold U.S. citizenship. Her father, Jun, had come to Seattle from Japan at the age of 17. In 1907, Jun returned to his native land to

*Iva Toguri (1916-1988), accused of being "Tokyo Rose,"
is led from a federal courtroom in 1949.*

marry Fumi Iimuro. Then he sailed back to the United States to work at various jobs while his wife remained in Japan. Not until 1913 did Fumi join her husband in San Francisco, where Iva was born three years later.

When Iva was a toddler, the family moved near the California-Mexico border to raise cotton, but their venture failed. After living briefly in San Diego, the Toguris eventually settled in Los Angeles in 1928. There, Jun Toguri finally established a small but successful import business.

Although the United States refused to grant American citizenship to Jun and Fumi because of bias against Asians, the Toguris tried hard to fit into the mainstream of American society, and they were proud that their daughter was an American by birth. Iva joined the Girl Scouts, took piano and tennis lessons, and celebrated her birthday on the Fourth of July with fireworks.

In June 1941, shortly after Iva graduated with a degree in zoology from UCLA, the family received a letter from Japan. Fumi Toguri's only sister, whom Fumi had not seen in nearly 30 years, was ill and wanted desperately to see Iva's mother before she died.

Fumi Toguri, however, was not well enough to travel, so the family sent Iva instead. Unfortunately, Iva was a victim of bureaucratic red tape. Instead of giving her a passport, the U.S. State Department issued her a certificate of identification authorizing her to stay in Japan for up to six months.

Iva sailed for Japan in July 1941. Upon arriving, she felt like an unwanted foreigner and warned her parents never to return to Japan. By December, the homesick young woman was eager to go back to California. But because she had no passport, she was unable to book passage on a ship bound for the United States.

On December 7, 1941, Japan attacked the U.S. naval base at Pearl Harbor, Hawaii. Japan and the United States were now at war, and Toguri was one of 10,000 Japanese Americans caught in Japan.

In their surprise attack on Pearl Harbor, the Japanese destroyed 19 ships and 188 aircraft, killed 2,280 soldiers and sailors, and wounded 1,109 more.

After the Japanese classified Toguri as an enemy alien, the police visited her several times a week, pressuring her to become a Japanese citizen. Toguri refused. She made no secret of the fact that she was loyal to the United States and expected the country of her birth to win the war.

Toguri's patriotism made her an embarrassment to her aunt and uncle. Neighbors taunted her and children threw stones at her. Toguri decided to find her own place to stay so her relatives could live in peace.

To make money, Toguri accepted a position at a news agency. Her job was to listen to short-wave radio and pick up news of Allied troop movements. But the hours were bad and the pay was low. In August 1943, she found part-time work as a typist in the business office of Radio Tokyo. There, she corrected the grammar in the English-language scripts of propaganda programs that the Japanese were broadcasting to Allied troops.

Still open about her support for the United States, Toguri made friends with Allied prisoners of war (POWs), whom the Japanese forced to participate in the propaganda broadcasts. The POWs wanted to sabotage the Japanese broadcasts, so they wrote bad scripts laced with wording like "the planes took to their heels." While sounding reasonable to someone with a poor command of English, the phrases would sound ridiculous to Americans.

One of the POWs, Australian major Charles Cousens, suggested that Toguri take over reading some of the scripts on the air. He chose her because he knew she was someone whom he could trust to keep the POWs'

By the time Toguri began working at Radio Tokyo, her family, along with the other Japanese Americans on the West Coast, had been relocated to internment camps like this one at Tule Lake in northern California. The U.S. government feared that these citizens might spy for the Japanese.

subtle sabotage of the propaganda a secret. Also, her voice was so harsh and grating that Allied soldiers would see her show as a satire of the propaganda effort.

At first, Toguri wanted nothing to do with the propaganda broadcasts. But Cousens assured her that "her job would be purely and simply the reading of the script" that he and two other POWs would write for her. In November 1943, Toguri finally accepted the assignment as hostess of "Zero Hour." At her friends' suggestion, she called herself "Orphan Anne."

The scripts Toguri read between the musical selections were a comic form of flirting. "Cheerio once again to all my favorite family of boneheads," Toguri started her program. She called herself "your favorite enemy" and made outrageous comments, such as telling the American troops that she would lull them to sleep before sneaking up on them with her deadly nail file!

By that time, in addition to 12 other broadcasts hosted by women at Radio Tokyo, at least 9 other pro-Japanese stations throughout Asia aired similar programs with women announcers. American soldiers referred to all of these female Japanese disc jockeys as "Tokyo Rose." In fact, the nickname had become common among Allied soldiers before Toguri ever spoke a word on the air. No one knows where the name came from, but stories of the seductive Tokyo Rose grew in the soldiers' imaginations.

Allied soldiers in the Pacific had plenty to fear from the Japanese. The USS Yorktown, *attacked by Japanese fighter pilots in the Battle of Midway, sank on June 7, 1942.*

Toguri held her job at Radio Tokyo throughout the war. When Japan surrendered in August 1945, she wept with relief. Now at last she could return home to see her family and introduce them to her new husband, Felipe d'Aquino, a Portuguese citizen of Japanese descent she had met while the two worked at the news agency.

Meanwhile, American reporters arrived in Tokyo, determined to find the legendary Tokyo Rose. Officials at Radio Tokyo denied that such a person existed. They pointed out that the "Zero Hour" program alone had used five or six female announcers, and none ever went by the name Tokyo Rose. But when reporter Clark Lee discovered that Iva Toguri had been one of the women broadcasting at Radio Tokyo, he filed a story identifying her as one of the women known as Tokyo Rose.

Another reporter working with Lee offered Toguri $2,000 for an exclusive interview for *Cosmopolitan* magazine. Toguri never imagined that her performance on "Zero Hour" might be treason. In fact, she believed that she had boosted the morale of American soldiers by providing them with music and a few laughs. The fuss reporters were making over Tokyo Rose convinced her that she was the idol of American soldiers. Naively, she signed a contract in which she confessed to being "the one and original" Tokyo Rose.

All Iva Toguri got from the contract was trouble. The magazine had not authorized a fee for the interview and refused to pay it. Then, on September 17, 1945, U.S. military police arrested Toguri without a warrant on suspicion of treason and held her in prison for months.

The press stopped referring to her as *a* Tokyo Rose. Now she was *the* Tokyo Rose. Still unaware of the seriousness of her predicament, Toguri complied when visitors to her cell asked her to sign autographs as Tokyo Rose.

At the time of Toguri's arrest, the U.S. Office of War Information knew that no single Tokyo Rose existed. By April 1946, investigators reported finding no evidence that Toguri had done anything wrong. Civil courts in the United States also cleared Toguri of any wrongdoing. The office of the U.S. attorney general issued a statement saying that "Toguri's activities, particularly in view of the innocuous nature of her broadcasts, are not sufficient to warrant her prosecution for treason." Despite these conclusions, the War Department did not release her from prison until October 25, 1947.

Toguri was relieved that the ordeal was over. At last she could return to the U.S. and be with her family, although her mother had died while Iva was in Japan. Iva's husband, however, thought that she should wait to go home until the publicity over Tokyo Rose had died down. Insisting that she had done nothing wrong, Iva ignored her husband's advice. She was pregnant and wanted her baby to be born in the United States.

Again, Toguri misjudged the situation. Veterans groups, particularly the American Legion, protested the return of the infamous Tokyo Rose, and influential radio broadcaster Walter Winchell demanded that the U.S. government try Toguri for treason. Afraid of appearing soft and unpatriotic as the presidential election neared, the Truman administration yielded to the demands.

The most popular journalist of his day, Walter Winchell wrote newspaper columns and made weekly radio broadcasts that reached well over 20 million people. When he decided Iva Toguri should be prosecuted, the government had little choice but to listen.

In August 1948, the U.S. Department of Justice again arrested Toguri. Her trial began almost a year later on July 5, 1949, in San Francisco, California. The government charged her with eight counts of treason. Because of its length and the fact that witnesses had to be flown in from overseas to testify, the three-month trial was the most expensive in the history of any U.S. federal court up to that time.

The prosecutors produced Toguri's signed confession admitting that she was Tokyo Rose and brought 19 witnesses from Japan to testify against her. Toguri's cooperation with Radio Tokyo, argued the lawyers for the prosecution, was clearly an act of aiding the enemy.

As proof that the broadcasts were intended to destroy the morale of American soldiers, the prosecutors cited a specific program that followed a battle at Leyte Gulf in the Philippines. According to the prosecution, Toguri had taunted the Americans by saying, "Orphans of the Pacific, you are really orphans now. How will you get home now that your ships are sunk?"

Most reporters covering the trial thought the prosecution's case was flimsy. Cousens and other POWs for whom Toguri had worked had all been cleared of treason, so how could someone who simply read what they had written for her be convicted? Cousens felt so strongly about Toguri's innocence that he flew from Australia at his own expense to support her. Another POW, an American named Norman Reyes who had written many of Toguri's scripts, testified, "I would have trusted her with my life."

Furthermore, Toguri's confessions and autographs did not prove her guilt. How could she have been Tokyo Rose when that name was well known before she had ever broadcast a word? Reporters and American soldiers insisted that Toguri's voice was not the one they associated with Tokyo Rose. Even if it had been, soldiers never took any of her light banter seriously. They saw the whole "Zero Hour" show as the joke its POW creators had intended it to be.

On September 29, 1949, after more than 78 hours of deliberation, the jury found Toguri guilty of one of eight counts of treason for one of the programs she had announced. The court sentenced her to 10 years in prison and a $10,000 fine.

Historians are virtually unanimous in declaring Iva Toguri's case a gross miscarriage of justice. Japanese witnesses for the prosecution later reported that the U.S. government had pressured them into giving false testimony. "We had no choice," said one. "U.S. occupation police came and told me I had no choice but to testify against Iva or else." In addition, the defense was able to bring few overseas witnesses to testify to Toguri's innocence. Moreover, nonwhites were struck from the jury, and Toguri was tried in an atmosphere of intense anti-Japanese sentiment.

Toguri served 6 years and 2 months of her 10-year term, paying for the crimes of the legendary Tokyo Rose

Iva Toguri speaks with reporters after her release from prison on January 28, 1956.

In order to be allowed into the United States to testify at his wife's trial, Felipe d'Aquino had to pledge to return to Japan within six months. He left the country just one week after Iva's conviction.

and for her own naiveté. In 1956, she emerged from prison and rejoined her family in Chicago. Toguri's husband had been sent back to Japan, and she never saw him again. Sadder but wiser about the dangers of publicity, Toguri kept to herself and asked reporters to leave her alone. She claimed not to be bitter over the bad luck and hysteria that had made her the last American convicted for treasonous activities during World War II.

In fact, Toguri's only request was to be pardoned so she could regain the U.S. citizenship that meant so much to her even after all she had been through. In 1976, President Gerald Ford finally granted her request. His action allowed Iva Toguri to live the final 12 years of her life as a citizen of the United States.

Ethel and Julius Rosenberg sit separated by a heavy wire screen after their conviction for conspiracy to commit espionage against the United States.

5

Julius and Ethel Rosenberg
Selling the Atomic Bomb

On August 6, 1945, the United States dropped the first atomic bomb on Hiroshima, Japan. That single event made the U.S. the military master of the world, for its government alone possessed the knowledge to create this terrible weapon. Since no other nation could hope to stand against the power unleashed by the atomic bomb, the United States now believed there was nothing to fear from any enemy.

This invincibility lasted only four years until, on August 29, 1949, the Soviet Union tested its own atomic bomb. The American public learned of the Soviets' weapon a month later. Suddenly, their sense of security was shattered.

Then came an aftershock that left Americans aghast. Intelligence agents determined that someone had smuggled secrets to the Soviets to help them build their atomic bomb. A small ring of American spies appeared to have handed the powers of annihilation to the nation's most feared enemy. The accused organizers of this conspiracy were a harmless-looking couple named Julius and Ethel Rosenberg.

Julius, born in New York City in 1918, was the youngest in a family of five children. His father, Harry, had come to New York from Russia in 1902 to escape persecution of Jews. In pursuit of the American dream, the new immigrant worked long, exhausting hours in a clothing factory.

During Julius's childhood, his parents eked out a living in a poor neighborhood on the city's Lower East Side. As a union member, Harry Rosenberg took part in the garment workers' frequent strikes against low wages. Although Harry's wages sometimes rose after a strike, the family often went without enough food during those work stoppages.

While Julius was a teenager, the country slid into a deep economic depression. Times were rough for almost everyone. Julius sold candy to help his family make ends meet.

Julius's sense of justice had been sharpened by studying the Talmud, the book of Jewish law. The misery of the Great Depression left him disillusioned about the free-enterprise system of the United States. Ripe for some alternative, he happened to walk past a speaker on a street corner who was pleading for support for an imprisoned labor leader. The plea touched the 15-year-old's heart. He made a small contribution to the cause and took home a pamphlet that the speaker had given him.

After reading the brochure, Rosenberg became more determined than ever to fight for justice for the poor. Upon entering City College of New York in 1934 at the age of 16, he helped to organize a chapter of the American Student Union, a national organization that supported various left-wing causes. Along with many of his fellow students, Rosenberg also joined the Young Communist League. That decision disturbed his father, who was a staunch patriot.

Communism advocates the ownership of factories, businesses, and farms by their workers. Julius believed the creed offered the world's best hope for combating poverty, racism, and *anti-Semitism*, or prejudice against Jews. Like many Americans and Europeans of his generation, Rosenberg found another reason to embrace Communism in his opposition to Fascism, a militaristic, antidemocratic movement that was overtaking Italy, Germany (as Nazism), and Spain.

Ethel Greenglass, born in 1915, grew up in the same poor Jewish neighborhood as Julius Rosenberg. Her father worked in a basement repairing sewing machines. Ethel wanted to be an entertainer, but the family had no money for music or acting lessons, and her mother ridiculed her for wasting her time in school plays.

Determined to be independent, Ethel saved every penny she could from school lunches and bus fares until she was able to afford a second-hand piano. She won prizes in musical competitions and attracted notice as an actress in local theater productions. After graduating from high school, she worked as a secretary to pay for voice lessons. When she became the youngest singer in a professional choir called Schola Cantorum, her career seemed to be taking off. But she left the choir after a year because she could not leave her job to go on tour.

At her secretarial job with a freight-brokerage company, Ethel met members of the Young Communist League who shared her interest in the arts. Under their influence, she became a determined fighter for working people. In August 1935, the tiny 19-year-old helped to organize a strike of 150 shipping clerks. When replacement workers and hired thugs attacked the strikers, Ethel and thousands of other workers—who had joined the strike as sympathizers—took to the streets, marching and lying down on the pavement to block traffic. Although the strike accomplished little, it introduced Ethel to labor activism. Her employer tried to fire her for her increasing involvement in politics, but she filed an unfair labor-practice complaint against the company—and won.

Ethel soon became a popular performer at leftist political events. In December 1936, she sang at a union benefit attended by a wiry man who took an immediate interest in her. This was the first meeting of Julius Rosenberg and Ethel Greenglass. The pair quickly discovered they had much in common.

Julius and Ethel as a young, happy couple

Julius confided that because he was so far behind in his classes and so short of money, he planned to drop out of college. Ethel talked him out of quitting and offered to give up her singing career and help him by typing his papers. Even with Ethel's assistance, Julius was barely able to graduate near the bottom of his class in 1939. The two married that June.

When Julius found work as a civilian electrical engineer with the U.S. Army Signal Corps, he and Ethel continued to participate in Communist activities. Then, late in 1943, the couple suddenly quit their open involvement in the Party. Nevertheless, the Federal Bureau of Investigation (FBI) sent a warning to the army about Julius's sympathies the following year. In early 1945, the army fired him for having lied about his Communist past.

Julius had no luck in finding another permanent job that paid well. In late 1945, he started up a machine shop with Ethel's brothers Bernard and David Greenglass. David became the foreman of the shop after being discharged from the army. The business, which continually lost money, created hard feelings between David and Julius.

In 1949, the Soviets exploded their atomic bomb. Just over five months later, in February 1950, investigators discovered from decoded Soviet messages that English scientist Klaus Fuchs was a spy. Fuchs confessed to betraying atomic secrets during the time he had worked with American scientists on developing the atomic bomb. Information from his confession provided clues as to who else was involved in the betrayal.

Authorities followed the trail of treachery to the door of Philadelphia chemist Harry Gold. In May, Gold confessed to being in on the plot to betray the most important secret in history.

Gold steered police to yet another conspirator, former army machinist David Greenglass. Greenglass immediately named his brother-in-law, Julius Rosenberg, as the leader of the spy ring. Eventually, Greenglass implicated his sister, Ethel, in the plot as well.

In 1935, Harry Gold began providing the Soviet Union with chemical formulas for industrial products. Gold wanted to help what he saw as an important and historic socialist experiment.

As in the Hiss case, the government could not charge the Rosenbergs with treason, the crime that was on everyone's lips. In the United States, treason is the act of aiding a country with which the United States is at war. For the brief time during which the spies gave atomic secrets to the Soviets, the U.S. and the Soviet Union were allies. Therefore, the prosecution could charge the Rosenbergs only with conspiracy to commit espionage by obtaining government secrets.

Julius Rosenberg (left) was arrested on July 17, 1950, one month after David Greenglass accused him of recruiting spies for the Soviet Union.

The trial of Julius and Ethel Rosenberg began on March 6, 1951, in the most hostile of environments. The American public boiled with rage because traitors had given the Soviets' ruthless dictator, Josef Stalin, the ultimate weapon. The fact that the U.S. was now involved in a war in Korea against Korean Communists who were Soviet allies made matters all the worse.

As in the Alger Hiss trial, the prosecution's case rested primarily on the statements of one man, David Greenglass, who had worked as a machinist in an army shop in Los Alamos, New Mexico, where components of the atomic bomb were built. The spectacle of a man testifying against his own sister on such a serious charge intensified the drama.

Greenglass claimed that Julius Rosenberg had supplied the Soviets with military secrets that he had learned as an electrical engineer on army projects. According to Greenglass, Julius had also boasted of photographing secret documents about guided missiles and aircraft.

Continuing his testimony, Greenglass stated that in 1944, a year after he had joined the army, he was sent to New Mexico to work on the secret bomb that the Americans were developing in the desert. He did not actually know the nature of the secret project until Julius recruited him to supply information to the Soviets.

According to Greenglass, his brother-in-law took elaborate precautions when he arranged meetings between Greenglass and Harry Gold, who would send the secrets on to the Soviets. For example, Rosenberg gave Greenglass half of a panel from a Jell-O box and

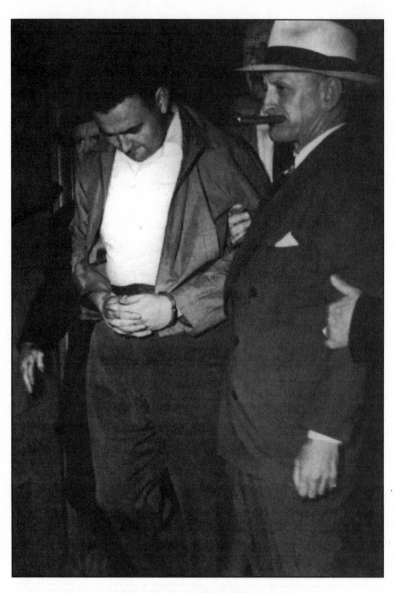

David Greenglass (left) leaves federal court on June 16, 1950, after confessing to the FBI. At first he resisted testifying against his relatives, but his lawyers convinced him to cooperate with the government in the hope of getting a reduced sentence.

told him that his contact in New Mexico would be the person who presented him with the matching half. That man turned out to be Gold. Gold's testimony backed up Greenglass's version of the events.

Greenglass testified that while he was on vacation in New York in September 1945, he visited the Rosenbergs' home. While there, he sketched out and wrote a description of the components of the atomic bomb. According to Greenglass, Ethel typed up the description in the Rosenbergs' living room.

At the end of the war, Greenglass left the army and returned to New York, where he and his brother-in-law went into business together. According to Greenglass, Julius asked him to continue spying through his army contacts, but Greenglass refused. Then, when Julius heard of Klaus Fuchs's arrest, he urged Greenglass to leave the country.

Greenglass told the court that when Fuchs led the authorities to Gold, Julius grew hysterical, knowing that agents were closing in on him and his wife. He gave Greenglass $5,000 and told him to get passport photos. He had plotted an escape that would take Greenglass to Czechoslovakia while Julius and Ethel went into hiding in the United States.

Ruth Greenglass supported her husband's testimony. When the government assigned David to the secret New Mexico facility, she had stayed in New York. She told the court that Julius had dropped out of Communist Party activities sometime during World War II so that he could work undercover as a Communist agent. She testified that Julius had told her about David's work on the atomic bomb over dinner one night at the Rosenbergs' home. Julius, she claimed, had insisted the world would be in grave danger if the United States was the only country with the bomb. Julius believed that David would be doing humanity a great favor by sharing classified information about the weapon.

A few other bits of evidence reinforced the prosecution's case. Morton Sobell, a friend of Julius Rosenberg who was also being tried in this case, had fled the country when the spy ring began to unravel. And Julius had made inquiries about overseas vaccinations at the time he was reportedly urging Greenglass to leave the country.

Under orders by the FBI, Morton Sobell was kidnapped in Mexico and brought back to the United States to stand trial with the Rosenbergs. He was sentenced to 30 years in prison.

Denying everything that Greenglass had said, Julius Rosenberg insisted, "I owe my allegiance to my country at all times." When the judge asked him whether he had belonged to any groups that discussed the Soviet Union's system of government, Rosenberg invoked the Fifth Amendment, refusing to answer on the grounds that he might incriminate himself. He denied knowing anything about the atomic bomb or about Greenglass's work on the project and claimed that Greenglass held a grudge against him because of a quarrel over their failed business venture.

Rosenberg testified that he had not given Greenglass $5,000 to flee the United States. Instead, Greenglass had demanded the money without giving Rosenberg a reason. Ethel backed up her husband's story.

The Rosenbergs' attorney, Manny Bloch, pointed out that there was little evidence against the Rosenbergs besides the testimony of Greenglass. As for Greenglass, Bloch blasted him as "the lowest of the lowest animals that I have ever seen." How could the jury trust the word of a man who would testify against his own sister in a case in which the death penalty was a possibility?

Behind the scenes of the trial, the Rosenbergs and the FBI were playing a high-stakes game of chicken. From Greenglass's statements and supporting testimony by Harry Gold, the FBI was convinced that Julius was the key figure in a large spy operation. How else could he have had knowledge of the secret bomb project? How else could he have known about Fuchs's arrest before the authorities had announced it? Yet Julius Rosenberg refused to talk.

To pressure Julius into confessing, the FBI had arrested Ethel, even though the evidence suggested that her role in the spying was small. Although Julius was devoted to his wife, her arrest did not made him talk. Now the prosecution decided to seek the death penalty for Julius. If he confessed, he could save his life. But both Julius and Ethel continued to maintain their innocence.

On March 29, 1951, the jury found Julius and Ethel Rosenberg guilty of conspiracy to commit espionage. A week later, Judge Irving Kaufman told the Rosenbergs that he held them personally responsible for allowing the

Arrested on August 11, 1950, Ethel Rosenberg was not even permitted to find someone to care for her two young sons before being imprisoned. She remained defiant throughout the ordeal.

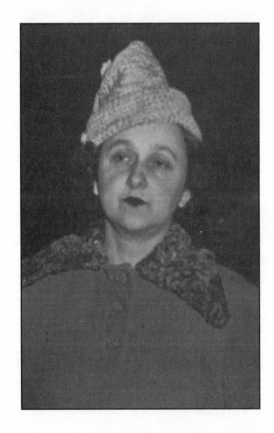

Manny Bloch, the Rosenbergs' lawyer, failed to damage the credibility of prosecution witnesses or to explain why they would frame an innocent couple. Still, Ethel and Julius Rosenberg never lost faith in their attorney.

Soviet Union and its allies to take a more aggressive role in the world. This aggression, he said, had led to such conflicts as the Korean War, in which American troops were risking their lives even as the trial was being held.

Because of the enormity of their crime, Kaufman sentenced both Julius and Ethel to die in the electric chair. The sentence stunned even the prosecutors. They had never dreamed that Ethel would be given the death penalty. After all, her only involvement in the crime appeared to have been typing a document and offering moral support to her husband. Moreover, of the more than two dozen Americans convicted of treason and espionage during World War II, none had been put to death.

Although J. Edgar Hoover, director of the FBI, was aware that Klaus Fuchs had given the Soviets the most damaging information on the bomb, he still called the Rosenbergs' actions "the crime of the century."

The government offered the Rosenbergs a last chance to confess and win a reduced sentence of life in prison, but the couple refused the offer.

Many historians suspect that the Rosenbergs were reluctant to betray friends who might have been involved with them. In any case, the Rosenbergs believed that "the people"—workers and leftists—would rise up and demand that their lives be spared. Calling for the public's sympathy, the Rosenbergs sought to have their verdict overturned or their death sentence suspended.

The Rosenbergs' lawyers argued that the sentence was unfair. None of the other people convicted of passing atomic secrets faced death. A jury had earlier convicted Harry Gold and David Greenglass of the same crime as the Rosenbergs. But Gold's sentence had been 30 years in prison, and Greenglass had received only 15.

Ruth Greenglass had been as much involved with her husband's activities as Ethel had been with Julius's, but Ruth had not even been charged in the case. Even Klaus Fuchs, who had given the Soviets far more accurate and important information than the Rosenbergs had provided, had received only 14 years from the British courts.

The Rosenbergs claimed to be victims of the new hostility of Americans towards the Soviet Union. "With the way things are in this country today, we would have been convicted if there was no testimony," Ethel charged. Their lawyers insisted that even if they had betrayed secrets—which the Rosenbergs continued to deny—they had not given these secrets to enemies of the United States. Regardless of how the United States and the Soviet Union viewed each other in 1951, they were allies at the time the espionage had allegedly taken place. The Rosenbergs had been tried for conspiracy but sentenced for treason.

These arguments made sense to many people. International figures, such as the scientist Albert Einstein and Pope Pius XII, pleaded with the United States government to spare the Rosenbergs' lives. All over the world, crowds demonstrated in their favor.

For two years, Ethel and Julius remained isolated in prison while their lawyers appealed to higher courts. But the courts declined to interfere with the case. President

Dwight D. Eisenhower, too, disregarded the public outcry over the sentences. "The nature of the crimes involves deliberate betrayal of the entire nation and the cause of freedom," he declared. He refused to exercise his power to *commute*, or reduce, the sentences to life in prison.

Neither side blinked in this war of nerves between the convicted couple and the government. As a result, the story of the Rosenbergs ended in a grim fashion. On June 19, 1953, Julius went to his death in the electric chair, still maintaining his innocence. On that same day, the government also executed his wife, Ethel.

President Dwight D. Eisenhower (1890-1969) believed that if he showed mercy to the Rosenbergs, Communist leaders around the world would conclude that democratic nations would not stand up to the Communist threat.

On August 6, 1945, the United States dropped the first atomic bomb, Little Boy, on Hiroshima, Japan. It was not long before the Soviet Union also had the power to use atomic weapons.

While few historians doubt that the Rosenbergs were guilty as charged, the harsh sentence continues to cast a dark cloud over the episode. Contrary to the popular notion at the time of the trial, the leaked secrets did not give the Soviet Union a weapon that it otherwise would never have had. In 1941 a British government commission concluded that any of the dominant countries of the world could develop an atomic bomb within three to four years with a concentrated effort. Even with information provided by spies, the Soviets completed their weapon no faster than scientists had predicted.

While the Rosenbergs indeed betrayed their country, they paid a far greater price than did traitors whose actions may have had much more serious consequences—as the following chapters show.

Described by his commanding officers as "intensely loyal," John Walker stole secrets from the U.S. Navy for 17 years to sell to the Soviet Union.

6

John Walker
Family Secrets

*T*he John Walker family had gone through its share of difficult times. In the first years of the Walkers' marriage, the family had bounced around the country as the U.S. Navy moved John from one assignment to the next. The family often had to scrimp to make his paycheck stretch to cover all their bills.

Recently, however, the financial pressure had eased. Although John made less than $20,000 a year as a naval officer and was losing money on a bar he owned, his family was no longer strapped for cash. On the contrary, John and his wife, Barbara, lived with their four children in a luxury apartment in Norfolk, Virginia, and drove expensive cars.

Barbara Walker had a nagging feeling that something was not quite right about these easy times. She also wondered why John went out so often in civilian clothes without telling her where he was going.

One night, her curiosity got the best of her. She snooped in John's desk drawer, looking for clues to what was going on in her husband's life. She found some film, maps, and photographs of a site where he was to leave information. She also discovered a letter saying the last delivery had not been up to expected standards.

For two weeks Barbara said nothing to her husband, but one night she exploded. "Traitor!" she accused John. "You're a spy!" But it would take her another 16 years to turn her husband over to the FBI.

John Anthony Walker Jr. was born on July 28, 1937, in Washington, D.C., to John and Peggy Walker. The family moved frequently, finally settling in Richmond, Virginia. While working as a salesman, John Sr. was nearly killed in a car collision in Maryland. The accident wiped out the family's savings. John Sr., who was an alcoholic, began to drink heavily, fight, and abuse his family.

John Jr., known then as Jack, grew to hate his father so much that he plotted to kill him. One night, Jack dragged a cast-iron rollaway bed to the top of the stairs and waited for his father to come home drunk. He intended to push the bed on top of his dad as he came up the stairs. But Jack fell asleep before his father arrived home, and he never had the courage to try again.

Scranton, Pennsylvania, as it looked in the late 1940s, when Jack Walker was beginning to get into trouble by throwing eggs at cars and setting fires

After losing their house because of missed payments, the Walker family moved to Scranton, Pennsylvania, to live with relatives. Jack was miserable. He hated both his home life and school. Eventually, he took out his frustrations by stealing money from neighborhood churches.

At the age of 12, Jack Walker once shot headlights out of cars on a highway. He robbed a gas station and tried to run away when police officers closed in on him. After Jack's arrest, his father was so angry that he left him in jail overnight rather than pay his bail. Jack was put on probation, and police suspected he was involved in at least 10 other burglaries.

Jack's older brother Arthur had escaped the nightmarish family situation by joining the navy. When he discovered the trouble Jack was getting into, he suggested his younger brother join him in the service. Arthur enjoyed navy life and believed the discipline would turn Jack around. Jack agreed, and the navy accepted him despite his criminal record and extremely poor eyesight.

As Arthur had predicted, Jack loved the service. Although he had shown no interest in his studies at St. Patrick's High School in West Scranton, Jack accepted the challenges the navy threw at him and studied hard to pass the requirements for promotions. Reports from his supervisors called him "superior" in all areas. To all observers, Jack was a patriotic young man.

In 1957, while he was stationed in Boston, Jack met 19-year-old Barbara Crowley at a skating rink. Barbara seemed to have a lot in common with Jack. She had hated living with her stepfather so much that she had left home on her eighteenth birthday.

That spring, Barbara became pregnant. She and Jack decided to get married, but they were too young to wed in Massachusetts without their parents' consent. So they traveled to North Carolina where regulations were less strict and became husband and wife on June 4, 1957.

John, as he now preferred to be called, held strong views about the roles of men and women. "The navy is my job," he told Barbara. "The house and the children are yours." But with three daughters by the end of their third year of marriage and her husband away at sea for long stretches, Barbara was often overwhelmed.

Scarred by his childhood poverty and abuse and determined not to repeat his father's mistakes, Walker saved every penny he could. His steady promotions gradually increased his salary, but he made a major mistake when he bought some property in Ladson, South Carolina, in 1966. He planned to open the Bamboo Snack Bar, but his partner backed out of the deal before the bar was ready for business, leaving John holding a large share of debt. Just before the bar finally began serving customers in September 1967, Walker was promoted to the rank of warrant officer and transferred to Norfolk, Virginia. Barbara stayed in Ladson and tried to manage the business as well as care for the family, but it was an impossible task. The bar steadily lost money, and Barbara took to drinking.

Too proud to admit a mistake, Walker would not sell the bar. Instead, he came up with a simple solution to his money problems. As a warrant officer at the operations headquarters of the U.S. Atlantic Fleet, he had access to crucial military secrets like the navy's strategy for conflicts in the Middle East or Central America and the workings of the sound surveillance system that tracked Soviet submarines. One night, Walker and another sailor jokingly had wondered what the Soviets would pay for such secrets. Now, on impulse, he decided to find out.

In December 1967, Walker stole a top-secret list that revealed how the navy set its code machines to change the code every 24 hours. Ironically, Walker's career as a spy nearly ended before it began when a coworker caught him making a photocopy of the

*The naval base in Norfolk, Virginia, where John
Walker began his career as a spy*

documents. But the fellow sailor did not check to see
what Walker was copying and simply scolded him for
using a navy copier for his own personal use.

Not long after the theft, Walker strode through the
door of the Soviet embassy in Washington, D.C., and
showed officials there the document he had stolen from
the navy. He offered to make a career of stealing secrets
for the Soviets in exchange for money. Suspicious at first,
the Soviets studied the document Walker had brought.
Recognizing how valuable it was, they immediately
handed him $1,000. The Soviet officials then made
arrangements to do further business with Walker.

In May, the U.S. nuclear submarine *Scorpion* sank off the Canary Islands while monitoring Soviet warships. John Walker was forced to ask himself whether information he had sold to the Soviets had led to the disaster. If so, how soon would it be before he was found out?

Barbara Walker, too, had doubts. She was glad that the family's living standards were changing for the better, but she did not believe John's story about making a lot of money by working a second, part-time job. When John finally leased his bar in Ladson in April 1968, she and the children joined him in Norfolk. It was there that Barbara broke into John's locked desk and discovered how he was getting the money he was using to support his family in their new luxury apartment.

When Barbara confronted him with his treachery, John gave her two black eyes. After he calmed down, he told her that his spying was no big deal. Many people did it. For the moment, Barbara accepted his explanation.

In autumn 1969, the navy transferred Walker across the country to San Diego, California. There he met Jerry Whitworth, a radio instructor at the Naval Training Center, whom he began to cultivate as a potential partner in espionage. After being recruited by Walker in 1974, Whitworth became one of the first government radio operators to work in the new field of satellite communications. He would provide Walker with information to sell to the Soviets after Walker retired from the navy.

Meanwhile, Walker realized that he would have less access to secrets in San Diego than he had in Norfolk. He also wanted to get away from his miserable marriage. In

1971, he applied for duty in Vietnam, where the U.S. was at war with Soviet-backed forces in the north. On the USS *Niagara Falls*, Walker became the officer responsible for the ship's *cryptographic*, or encoding, materials. His value to the Soviets once again soared. In this post, he would shamelessly coordinate rescue missions for U.S. pilots that his treachery had helped shoot down.

In 1975, Walker was transferred back to Norfolk, where he started a business with his brother Arthur, whom he would also recruit into the spy ring. Barbara had wanted to leave him, but John, worried that if they divorced she would turn him in, persuaded her to return to Norfolk with him.

By this time, Walker had convinced himself that he was the best secret agent in the business. He had out-smarted the U.S. government, and he believed he would never be prosecuted even if the government somehow managed to catch on to him. His connections with the Soviets were so valuable that U.S. officials would simply ask him to play double agent and feed the Soviet Union false information.

When he returned to Norfolk, Walker continued to spy for the Soviets, making "drops" of stolen informa-tion to hidden locations in the countryside around Washington, D.C. Between 1968 and 1985, he made at least 30 such deposits. To make it harder for Barbara to turn him in, he once even enlisted her help in making a drop. Barbara debated telling the FBI about her hus-band on at least four occasions, but she always backed down for fear of hurting their children.

Barbara finally found the courage to leave John in 1976. She filed for divorce and moved with their children to Maine. In 1980, to Barbara's anguish, their 18-year-old son, Michael, decided to move back with his father. She was well aware of both her husband's ability to talk people into doing things and Michael's eagerness to please his father. Because she had feared that Michael might fall into one of her ex-husband's schemes, Barbara was relieved when Michael joined the U.S. Navy in 1982. She didn't realize that joining the navy put Michael into a position to spy. His father recruited him within a year.

John Walker was thrilled when, in January 1984, his son Michael was assigned to the USS Nimitz, the largest aircraft carrier in the U.S. naval fleet.

By this time John Walker had retired from the navy and started a detective agency in Virginia Beach, Virginia. But his navy contacts, including his son and Jerry Whitworth, continued to feed him classified information to sell to the Soviets. On one occasion, when passing this information involved traveling to Europe in disguise, Walker's Soviet contact urged him to read the popular detective novel *The French Connection* for tips on spying!

Bankrolled by his Soviet clients, John Walker enjoyed a flashy lifestyle that included a houseboat, young girlfriends, an airplane, and trips around the world. Meanwhile, Barbara worked long shifts in a shoe factory in Maine to support herself.

In 1984, one of the Walkers' daughters, Laura, came to her mother in desperation. After she joined the U.S. Army in 1978, Laura told Barbara, her father had tried to recruit her for his spy ring. Laura had refused, but she had told her husband about her father's request. When Laura and her husband separated, he kidnapped their son. Now he threatened to turn in his father-in-law to the government if Laura tried to get their son back.

When she saw that John's treason was beginning to destroy one of her children's lives, Barbara took action. She called the Federal Bureau of Investigation (FBI) in November 1984 to tell the agency what she knew about her ex-husband's activities. The FBI, however, did not believe her. Even when Laura supported her mother's story, the agency delayed checking their information. Finally, in the spring of 1985, the FBI looked into the case and found that Walker was indeed acting suspiciously.

On May 19, 1985, John Walker drove from Norfolk, Virginia, to a rural area just outside Washington, D.C. He carried with him a white plastic trash bag containing his latest batch of more than 100 secrets he had obtained from his navy contacts. Out in the countryside, Walker stopped and set a 7-Up can on the edge of the road to signal his Soviet contacts that he was making a drop. He then placed the trash bag of secrets near a telephone pole and drove on. Soon Walker reached the second pre-arranged point, where Soviet intelligence officers, posing as diplomats at the Soviet embassy, were to leave the money they were paying him. Walker expected to net more than $200,000 for his latest bundle of information. But when he reached the second drop point, the money was not there.

Confused, Walker returned to his hotel to review his packet of instructions from the Soviets. Unknown to him, the FBI had followed him when he made his drop and agents had collected the bag of secrets. They had also picked up the 7-Up can, thinking it might contain film. The Soviets, not seeing the signal that everything was okay, had left without depositing Walker's payment.

Walker knew that something was wrong when the hotel clerk woke him up with a request that he come down to the lobby. When the FBI surrounded him in the hallway, he grinned and drew his gun. But he was outnumbered. The FBI placed him under arrest.

After 17 years of successful spying, Walker had gotten careless. The bag he had left for the Soviets included a letter that Walker had signed and information that the

FBI could use to track down other members of Walker's spy ring. The ring included John's brother, Arthur, who was a former instructor in antisubmarine warfare for the navy, and John's best friend, Jerry Whitworth, now retired from the navy.

Walker's carelessness also led to the capture of a fourth member of the spy ring—his son, Michael. From his post aboard the aircraft carrier USS *Nimitz*, Michael had been able to obtain naval secrets that none of John Walker's other contacts could get. Michael told the FBI that he had wanted to get out of the spy business, but he did not know how to say no to his father.

Nearly all the incriminating documents John Walker was delivering when he was arrested by the FBI had been stolen from the USS Nimitz *by his son Michael.*

Jerry Whitworth (right) had been trying unsuccessfully to get out of the spying business since 1981, the year John Walker had first managed to get classified information from his older brother Arthur (left), who was working for VSE Corporation, a defense contractor in Norfolk.

Barbara Walker was shocked when, a week after her husband's arrest, she saw her son in handcuffs on the network news. She later wrote that she would never have exposed her husband had she known that Michael was also involved in the spying.

In August 1985, Arthur Walker was put on trial. The court sentenced him to life in prison plus a $250,000 fine. After learning of his brother's severe punishment, John Walker agreed to cooperate with the authorities. He pleaded guilty to charges of supplying the Soviets

Barbara Walker (right) and daughter Cynthia leave the courtroom after John was sentenced to life in prison and Michael to 25 years. Cynthia had feared that her father would try to make her a spy, too.

with classified military secrets and offered testimony against Jerry Whitworth, the government's weakest case. In exchange, the government agreed to more lenient sentences for John and his son.

Jerry Whitworth received a life sentence and a $410,000 fine. The court sentenced John to a life sentence and Michael to 25 years in prison.

John Walker personally pocketed at least $750,000 from the information he had sold. Among the secrets he betrayed were American defense plans against submarine attacks, U.S. techniques for listening to and locating submerged Soviet submarines, and methods of hiding U.S. submarines from Soviet detection. These disclosures had helped the Soviets to improve their submarine fleet.

The spy ring's most serious treason, however, was the betrayal of codes used by American warships. This knowledge had allowed the Soviets to decipher hundreds of thousands of coded secret messages, including information on troop movements during the Vietnam War. The Soviets also knew where to locate American submarines if war began. They even knew the codes needed to launch U.S. nuclear missiles.

The activities of Walker's spy ring could have been disastrous for the United States. According to intelligence historian Chapman Pincher, "Had there been a war [with the Soviet Union] during the time that the Walker ring was active, the U.S. Navy would almost certainly have suffered heavy losses in life and ships." Pincher maintains that even in peacetime, the damage the Walkers inflicted on the U.S. was costly and might be "impossible to rectify."

Yet John Walker still considered himself a model American. "I'm very patriotic," he claimed. He also showed little remorse for his crimes, saying "Except for this one black mark, I've led a very impressive life." In fact, he thought of himself as a superspy and blamed the "weak people" around him for his downfall. If not for these "misfits," he bragged, the FBI would never have caught him.

Having shown his cleverness by getting away with his crime for 17 years, Walker expected that his arrest would make him a celebrity. Instead, history remembers him only as a man without a conscience—and one of the most despicable traitors in U.S. history.

*Edward Lee Howard takes a stroll in Moscow in
March 1985. He fled to the Soviet Union to escape
what he considered to be unfair persecution for spying.*

7

Edward Lee Howard
The Getaway

*E*dward Lee Howard maintains that he never betrayed the interests of the United States, and the U.S. government has never convicted nor even tried him for treason. But the lack of a trial has more to do with Howard's skill as a spy than with a lack of evidence that he had exposed secrets of the U.S. Central Intelligence Agency (CIA). The problem was that the CIA had taught Howard too well. Using what he had learned as an agent, Howard slipped through its fingers in a dramatic escape. Edward Howard holds the distinction of being the only member of the CIA ever to defect to the Soviet Union.

Edward Lee Howard was born in New Mexico in 1951. His father worked as an electronics specialist in the U.S. Air Force. Like John Walker's family, the Howard family learned that home was wherever the military wanted them. Edward spent much of his childhood in Germany and England, where he finished high school. Then he returned to the United States to attend the University of Texas at Austin.

After graduating from college with honors, Howard saw no reason to settle down in the States. Instead, he joined the Peace Corps and traveled to Colombia, South America. There, in 1973, he met an American coworker named Mary Cedarleaf. The two married in 1976.

After earning a master's degree in business from American University in Washington, D.C., Howard went back to South America—this time to Lima, Peru—to work on a loan project for an international development agency. Upon finishing the two-year assignment, he again returned to the United States. He took an office job working for a company specializing in environmental concerns, but he had barely settled into the work when the urge for adventure swept over him yet again. In 1980, he applied for a position with the CIA.

Howard was exactly what the CIA was looking for—a highly educated, conservative young man with no involvement in radical groups. His fluency in Spanish and German made him especially attractive to the government agency. As added bonuses, Howard knew how to care for and use a gun, and both he and his wife enjoyed living overseas.

Edward Howard was hired by the CIA in January 1981. In the autumn of that same year, Mary Howard also joined the agency. The couple spent more than a year in intensive training on the craft of spying. Early in 1982, the CIA selected the Howards for a top-secret assignment in Moscow, the capital of the Soviet Union. While Edward posed as a U.S. diplomat, he and Mary would work as a team, gathering intelligence information for the CIA.

The assignment was a dangerous one for a couple with no previous experience in spying. But the CIA's counterpart in the Soviet Union, the KGB, had information on many of the CIA's veteran agents, so the agency needed new recruits whom the KGB could not identify.

William Casey, director of the CIA in 1982, said that sending an inexperienced agent such as Howard to the Soviet Union was standard practice.

In March 1983, Mary and Edward Howard were ready to take on their mission. Their newborn son gave them an even more innocent appearance as a diplomat and his family.

Because of the sensitive nature of intelligence work, the CIA requires all operatives to take a final lie detector test before it trusts them in the field. After Howard's first test, he was asked to take several more. The tests turned up two red flags: he had used drugs, and he had once committed an act of petty theft.

Given this information, the CIA decided that it could not trust Howard with such a delicate assignment. But instead of finding a less important post for Howard, CIA officials fired him. The agency ran an unnecessary risk by treating Howard so harshly. During his training, the CIA had given him important classified information about the agency's Moscow operation. A person who was furious with the CIA might be tempted to use such secrets to get even.

Sure enough, Edward Howard wanted revenge against the CIA. In October 1983, he stood outside the Soviet embassy in Washington, D.C., trying to summon the courage to tell officials there what he knew. Although treason was still too terrible a notion for him at that time, Howard told two friends who worked for the government that he had thought seriously about passing secrets to punish the United States for his treatment. These friends recognized the possible danger to the CIA and reported to their superiors what Howard had said to them. The CIA, however, ignored the information.

Howard had no difficulty in finding another job, this time as an economic analyst for the New Mexico state legislature. So he and Mary, who left the CIA after her husband was fired, moved to Santa Fe, New Mexico. Howard's primary task was to estimate the amount of money the state could expect to raise through taxation.

On February 26, 1984, Edward Howard became involved in exactly the kind of incident that the CIA had feared would happen if the agency let him go to Moscow. While under the influence of alcohol one night in Santa Fe, he got into an argument with three youths. The argument escalated and Howard pulled a gun, firing a bullet through the roof of the car that the young men had been driving.

After the three wrestled the gun away from Howard and beat him up, the police arrested Howard on charges of assault with a deadly weapon. In exchange for his admission of guilt, Howard was able to work out a plea bargain in which the court fined him $7,500. He was also placed on probation and was ordered into counseling for alcohol abuse.

Over the next year Howard managed to keep a low profile. But in August 1985 a high-ranking KGB official named Vitaly Yurchenko defected to the United States. One of the first questions officials asked him was whether he knew of any Soviet spies operating in the United States. Yurchenko knew of two. One was Ronald Pelton. Following up on this lead, in November the Federal Bureau of Investigation (FBI) arrested Pelton. The U.S. government convicted him of espionage in May 1986.

Vitaly Yurchenko is now thought to have been a "fake" defector, sent by the KGB to give the CIA false or misleading information.

Yurchenko knew the other spy only by the code name "Robert." But he offered two clues to Robert's identity: the man had been trained for a CIA post in Moscow and had met with KGB officers in Austria.

The CIA and FBI immediately suspected Howard. When their investigation found that he had flown to an Austrian ski resort in September 1984, they were convinced that Howard had betrayed the United States.

Unfortunately, the case against Howard consisted of the testimony of a Soviet traitor and some flimsy circumstantial evidence—testimony that would not hold up in court. The U.S. government needed something more on Howard before it could make an arrest.

In late August 1985, the FBI placed Howard's house in Santa Fe under surveillance. At the same time, agents conducted an investigation that led them to Texas, where they located a man named William Bosch. Like Howard, Bosch had been dismissed rather abruptly from the CIA. When questioned, Bosch told the FBI that Howard had admitted to him that he had sold secrets to the Soviets. Furthermore, Howard had tried to recruit Bosch as a Soviet spy. That was all the FBI needed to hear. They prepared to arrest Howard.

Meanwhile, Howard had become aware that the FBI was watching his house. Even as the FBI was interviewing Bosch, Howard was making plans to flee the United States. One blazing hot afternoon in September 1985, Mary and Edward Howard drove away from their house in their red 1979 Oldsmobile. After eating at a restaurant, they returned to the car. Mary took the wheel and Edward climbed in the passenger seat.

Then they pulled a trick they had learned in the CIA. Lying on the floor of the car, Howard propped up a dummy wearing a baseball cap. As Mary took a tight turn in a downtown area, Howard rolled out of the slow-moving car and scurried away. Mary continued driving with the dummy sitting next to her.

When she returned to her home, it was dark. As she drove into her garage, the agents watching the house assumed that the figure beside Mary was her husband. For added effect, Mary took advantage of the fact that the FBI was tapping the Howard telephone line. To convince listeners that her husband was home, she dialed a business office and played a tape of Edward's voice leaving a message on the office's answering machine.

William Webster, director of the FBI when Howard fled the United States, called his escape an "aberration."

By the time the FBI moved in to arrest Howard, its quarry was long gone. Howard didn't surface until eight months later in Moscow, far out of the reach of American law enforcement.

Howard's Soviet hosts treated him well. He lived under 24-hour-a-day protection in a comfortable apartment in a KGB village west of Moscow. But he paid a price for the arrangement. He had to live away from his wife and son, who had stayed behind in the United States and could visit him only occasionally. Furthermore, the intense security designed to protect him from the CIA also made him a virtual prisoner in the village.

In the early 1990s, when the Soviet Union dissolved and the Communist Party fell from power, Howard began to worry. As relations between the Russians and the Americans improved, he wondered whether his hosts would turn him over to the United States as a gesture of good will. He was also unhappy because he desperately wanted to be with his wife and son, and Mary refused to live in Russia.

In December 1991, the Howards arranged a compromise. Edward risked moving to Stockholm, Sweden, where he ran a business exporting Swedish consumer goods to Russia in exchange for timber. His family joined him at Christmas. The FBI, however, quickly discovered the move and demanded that Howard return to the United States to face charges.

The federal agency could not arrest Howard in Sweden. Nor would Sweden, although on friendly terms with the United States, turn him over to the Americans. Like most countries, Sweden considered espionage to be a political crime—a quarrel between an individual and his or her government. Few nations want to become involved in such disputes, and so they seldom *extradite*, or hand over, political fugitives to the country they have fled.

Sweden did find a way to help the United States, however. On August 20, 1992, Swedish police arrested Edward Howard as he and his family were crossing a street in downtown Stockholm. In jail, he learned that he was accused of spying against Sweden. Rather than attempt to fight these charges, Howard reluctantly returned to Russia.

Howard has always claimed to be a victim of CIA persecution. "I love my country," he said shortly after his defection. "I have never done anything that might harm my country." Howard told a reporter that he defected and continued to stay in Russia only because he believed he could not get a fair trial in the United States. Mary Howard backed up his claim, saying that she had no reason to believe he had ever spied for the Soviets.

Some of Howard's supporters believe the Soviets framed him. Yurchenko, the man who "exposed" him, returned to the Soviet Union only a few months after he defected, so those who buy Howard's story wonder whether Yurchenko's accusations during his supposed defection were Soviet attempts to divert attention away from their real spies.

On the other hand, as evidence of payment for secrets, the FBI pointed to $10,000 Howard had buried in the New Mexico desert and to $150,000 he had stashed away in a Swiss bank. Furthermore, why were the Soviets so protective of him if he had never spied for them?

According to former CIA head Stansfield Turner, Howard had critical information about the agency's operations in Moscow, which were severely damaged shortly after Howard's trip to Austria. Among the most tragic consequences was the plight of Adolf Tolkachev.

Tolkachev, a Soviet engineer, was an expert on military stealth technology. A secret agent of the United States, he provided the CIA with Soviet military secrets. Howard knew about Tolkachev, and the Soviets executed the engineer shortly after Howard defected.

The FBI was shamefaced because Edward Lee Howard, shown here on his 1985 "wanted" poster, had escaped arrest.

Although some of the betrayals first attributed to Howard were subsequently pinned on Aldrich Ames, experts still believe that Howard turned in Tolkachev to the Soviets. Thus, it seems likely that if the defector Yurchenko was framing Howard, he was framing a lesser spy, not a completely innocent man.

The U.S. government believes that Edward Howard betrayed his country. The fact that it cannot prosecute Howard for that crime in a court of law has frustrated officials to no end. Edward Howard remains the "spy who got away."

More recent events, however, have overshadowed Howard's importance to the CIA, which once regarded him as the greatest embarrassment in the agency's history. In 1994, a new and more devastating humiliation surfaced in the form of Aldrich Ames.

*Aldrich Ames leaving a federal courthouse in March 1994,
a few weeks after being arrested as a spy*

134

8

Aldrich Ames
The Deadliest Mole

*I*n the autumn of 1985, Soviet nationals whom the U.S. Central Intelligence Agency (CIA) had recruited to spy for the United States began to disappear one by one. The Soviet government had begun to recall these "turned" agents from their posts abroad to face imprisonment or execution. By 1994, when the CIA discovered the cause of the purge, nearly three dozen agents had dropped out of contact. The Soviets had cleaned out virtually the entire CIA operation for gathering intelligence about the Soviet Union.

The CIA conducted an investigation to discover how such a disaster could have occurred. Far more agents had been knocked out of business than suspected traitor Edward Lee Howard could have known about from his brief stint in the CIA. The evidence pointed toward a "mole"—spy terminology for a traitor working within his or her country's headquarters.

The CIA, however, discounted the possibility that one of its dedicated, long-time employees could have stooped so low. The agency's report on the matter concluded that faulty or inadequate spy techniques had brought about the collapse of its Soviet operations.

But the report was wrong. A mole had indeed burrowed deep into the heart of the CIA. A trusted agent who had worked in the CIA for nearly 25 years was passing on top-secret information to the Soviet Union.

Rick Ames was not a superspy by anyone's estimate. His CIA superiors rated him as only a mediocre agent at best; some even considered him a lazy drunk. Yet he managed to elude detection while betraying more damaging secrets than any other traitor in U.S. history.

Aldrich Hazen Ames was born in the small town of River Falls, Wisconsin, on June 26, 1941, one of three children of Carleton and Rachel Ames. Carleton Ames taught history at River Falls Teachers' College, where his own father had served as college president. In 1951, the family pulled up their roots and moved from the Midwest to the Washington, D.C., area. There, Rachel Ames took a job as a classroom teacher while Carleton pursued a new career as an analyst with the CIA.

Rick, as Aldrich was known, attended high school in McLean, Virginia. After spending two years at the University of Chicago, he dropped out of school to follow in his father's footsteps by applying for a position as a trainee with the CIA. When he realized that only those with a college degree advance far within the CIA ranks, Ames resumed classwork at George Washington University in Washington, D.C., and graduated in 1967.

Carleton Ames never distinguished himself at the CIA; neither did his son. Rick Ames was sloppy in his work and careless about details. According to a colleague, Ames was "an incompetent, a goof-off who liked to have a good time." Ames's idea of a good time often involved

Carleton Ames worked for the CIA for 20 years, but his supervisors found him to be a troublesome employee with alcohol problems.

heavy drinking, but it seldom involved friends—because he did not have many.

Ames's first overseas mission took him to Ankara, Turkey. His chief accomplishment during his three years there as an undercover agent was finding a wife—Nancy, a fellow CIA agent whom he married in 1969.

Ames spent the 1970s back in the United States in Langley, Virginia, and New York City. One of his major assignments was to recruit Soviet workers at the United Nations to spy for the United States. As he got to know these workers, Ames realized that he was in an ideal position to make money by selling secrets to his new contacts. He could easily arrange meetings with Soviet agents because such secret contacts were part of his job.

In 1981, the CIA sent Ames to Mexico City. Ames's marriage had begun to unravel by this time, so he went alone. While in Mexico, he met a Colombian diplomatic aide named Maria del Rosario Casas Depuy. Ames put Casas Depuy on the CIA payroll as an informant. Although CIA rules specifically prohibited agents from getting romantically involved with foreign nationals, Ames soon fell in love with Casas Depuy.

The CIA believed in rewarding its people for long-time service. So the agency offered Ames a steady stream of promotions despite the fact that he had accomplished little in his two decades with the CIA, was known to have a drinking problem and marital problems, and had violated agency rules by becoming involved with Casas Depuy. In 1983, when Ames returned to the CIA headquarters at Langley, Virginia, the agency gave him one of

The Central Intelligence Agency was established in 1947 to gather information about other countries for the U.S. government.

its most sensitive positions: chief of the entire Soviet branch of counterintelligence. As chief, he directed the recruitment of Soviets into the CIA and set up ways of working with them as spies.

In 1985, the agency missed another warning sign that Ames was a security risk. Having recently divorced his first wife, he complained to colleagues that the divorce settlement had left him broke. Now he was not only short of cash, but he was also under pressure to provide for the woman who was giving up her homeland in Colombia to marry him.

Ames yielded to the pressure. In April, he sold the Soviets the names of two officers in the KGB—the Soviet equivalent of the CIA—whom the CIA secretly employed. Two months later, Ames wrapped up five pounds of classified documents in plastic bags and delivered them to Sergei Chuvakhin, a diplomat at the Soviet embassy in Washington, D.C. The package contained the largest collection of U.S. secrets ever betrayed. Inside the bags were the names of every Soviet intelligence and military officer who worked for the United States, along with vital information about U.S. spy operations.

Ironically, at about the same time he was entering the Soviets' service, Ames was one of those in charge of interrogating Vitaly Yurchenko, the KGB officer who had defected to the United States in August 1985. It was Yurchenko who had told the U.S. government that Edward Lee Howard was a Soviet spy.

Flush with his payoff—estimated at $50,000—Rick and Rosario married on August 10, 1985. That autumn, the CIA transferred Ames to the agency's station in Rome. There, he met repeatedly with KGB contacts, who would send a car to pick up Ames for a "business lunch." Ames would don a baseball cap, jacket, and dark glasses as the driver wound through the streets for 45 minutes, checking to see if someone was following them. Finally, Ames would meet his contact in a secret room. Their talks often lasted as long as five hours.

Normally, someone in the perilous position of a mole would be careful to avoid attracting attention. But Ames had never been particularly careful and old habits were hard to break. On one occasion, Ames got drunk at a reception for the U.S. ambassador in Rome and passed out in a gutter. Incredibly, the CIA overlooked even that embarrassment.

But to Ames's horror, the Soviet Union matched his carelessness. The KGB wasted no time in rounding up the "traitors" Ames had named. In 1986 and 1987, the Soviets executed Sergei Motorin and Valery Martynov, two of the U.S. government's most recent recruits. The stunned American intelligence community asked how the Soviets could have found out about the agents. Suspicion centered on Edward Lee Howard—who had defected in September 1985—but investigators determined that Howard could not have known about these two.

While the Americans were trying to track the source of Motorin and Martynov's exposure, the Soviet Union continued rounding up and executing spies. Ames was shocked and scared. The Soviets were all but announcing to the world that they had a mole in the CIA. How else could they have discovered that many agents all at once? To throw off suspicion, Ames thought the Soviets should arrest the spies slowly or even use them as a means to plant false information with the Americans.

In October 1986, CIA chiefs appointed a task force headed by Soviet expert Jeanne Vertefeuille to investigate the alarming disappearance of their Soviet agents. (Later, Vertefeuille would discover that Ames had asked the Soviet Union to frame *her* as the mole!) Fortunately for Ames, the probe turned up nothing, and the agency's analysts blamed poor tradecraft—sloppiness in carrying out secret operations—for all the blown covers. The FBI thought otherwise, but it could not conduct a thorough

William Webster left the FBI to become director of the CIA in 1988, but the agency still did not conduct a thorough search for a possible "mole."

investigation without CIA cooperation. Thus, Ames was free to continue selling secrets to the Soviets.

In November 1989, an employee at the CIA noticed that Rick Ames was living remarkably well for a person on a CIA salary. Furthermore, she observed, he had access to information that had been given to the Russians. But her superiors did not follow up on her suspicions. The Ames family—father and son—had been part of the CIA for more than 35 years. Because this family history implied a loyalty to the agency and its goals, CIA officials would not believe that Rick Ames was a traitor.

Rather than investigate Ames, the CIA installed him in another sensitive post in 1990. When Ames took over spy operations in western Europe, his job again involved contact with Russian embassies. In his new position, Ames could arrange meetings without suspicion and pass on to the Soviets whatever secrets he came across.

In April 1991, the growing number of operations that had been exposed finally convinced the CIA that the Soviets had a mole deep within the agency. So officials at the CIA approached the FBI and asked the federal law-enforcement organization to help the agency locate the traitor. (In the midst of these investigations, the Soviet Union collapsed in December 1991, but the Russians continued their espionage activities.)

The FBI launched one of the largest investigations in its history, involving as many as 100 full-time staff members. FBI agents compiled lists of everyone in the CIA with drinking, drug, money, or marital problems and everyone who had knowledge of any operations that had failed. The FBI agents did not know if they were dealing with one mole or several, but the sheer number of blown operations suggested more than one source of leaks.

After its initial probe, the FBI had a list of 200 suspects. Somehow, they needed to trim down this field without the mole knowing they were suspicious. Methodically, the FBI eliminated suspects from the list by checking out their access to revealed secrets. By October 1992, only 40 suspects remained out of the original 200.

Meanwhile, Rick Ames shamelessly catered to his expensive new tastes. In 1992, he bought his third Jaguar sports car. The more the list of suspects dwindled, the more Ames's careless behavior attracted interest. He had access to information about every agent who had been betrayed to the former Soviet Union. His drinking problems were no secret. He had paid cash for a house worth over one-half million dollars. How could he buy such an expensive house and three Jaguars on a salary of around $50,000 per year?

With the list of suspects trimmed again from 40 to 5, the FBI checked into Ames's bank records. They found he had made a large bank deposit right after a meeting with diplomat Sergei Chuvakhin. Rick Ames immediately jumped to the top of the suspect list.

The FBI began a full-scale investigation of Aldrich Ames on May 12, 1993. In June, the federal agency placed his home under surveillance and tapped his telephone. Ames, however, knew better than to conduct business near his home or to say much on the phone. For weeks, the FBI listened to his telephone conversations without learning anything of value.

On July 20, 1993, FBI agents secretly installed an electronic beacon in the red Jaguar Ames drove to work. This device allowed them to track Ames wherever he drove. But once again, Ames did nothing suspicious.

The next step was to search Ames's trash. Late on the night of September 15, 1993, a dark van quietly pulled up to the curb by Ames's house. Agents whisked away his trash can and replaced it with an identical one. Sifting through the garbage, one agent discovered a torn note that said "I am ready to meet at B— on 1 Oct." Agents discovered that Ames was scheduled to fly to Bogota, Colombia, at the beginning of October. That could mean he was bringing the Russians more information.

The FBI obtained a search warrant from Attorney General Janet Reno to enter Ames's home. In the early morning hours of October 9, 1993, while Ames was out of town with Rosario and their five-year old son, Paul, FBI agents sneaked into the house. They searched every room for clues.

Cracking into files in Ames's home computer, an FBI computer expert struck gold! Ames's files contained classified CIA information, notes about meetings with Russians, and detailed instructions about drop sites— places where Ames would leave or pick up messages.

The FBI and CIA were now certain they had found the mole, but they wanted to catch Ames in the act of

As the head of the Department of Justice, Janet Reno, the first woman to be appointed United States attorney general, was in charge of the FBI.

After Louis Freeh became director of the FBI in September 1993, he reorganized the "Nightmover" investigation of Aldrich Ames so the bureau could make a quicker arrest.

betrayal. When Ames left for Bogota on November 1—later than originally planned—14 security agents followed him, many of them carrying cameras to record any suspicious encounters he had while in South America. Although Ames had no idea that anyone was trailing him, he still managed to elude all his trackers long enough to meet secretly with a contact who gave him $125,000.

While FBI agents were puzzling over how they had missed their opportunity to seize Ames during his meeting with the Russians, Ames returned home. The FBI continued to try to catch him red-handed in treasonous acts, but Ames did nothing suspicious.

In January 1994, the FBI was horrified to learn that Ames had scheduled a flight to Moscow as part of legitimate CIA business. Scarred by the memory of Howard's getaway, the agency asked President Bill Clinton for help in keeping Ames in the United States. The White House staff responded by requesting a special CIA briefing on international drug traffic. The CIA asked Ames to head the presentation. Flattered, Ames postponed his Moscow trip until late February.

The FBI continued to wait and watch in the hope that Ames would make a major mistake. But when they detected an unusual number of Russian intelligence officers in Ames's neighborhood, they began to worry that someone would warn Ames about the investigation. Since they could not postpone Ames's trip a second time without suspicion, the FBI finally had to be content with the information it had.

On the morning of February 21, 1994, Ames backed his Jaguar out of the driveway and headed for his CIA office. Suddenly several cars blocked the road and hemmed him in. FBI agents rushed out of their cars and arrested Ames.

The FBI's worries that Ames would defect proved to be baseless. He had no idea that he was under suspicion and had no plans to leave the United States. In order to gain a reduced sentence for his wife, Rosario, who had been his accomplice in treason, Ames confessed to his crimes and cooperated with the FBI.

The news of Ames's arrest and reports of the damage he had inflicted on U.S. intelligence shocked the nation.

Trying to sift through the wreckage of the many operations Ames destroyed was almost impossible. But officials believe that he exposed as many as three dozen Soviet agents who were working for the U.S. government, at least 10 of whom were executed. The rest, CIA analysts believe, are in prisons or labor camps.

Like traitor John Walker, Ames's only motive was money. He collected well over $2 million for selling his secrets. In the words of CIA director James Woolsey, many men died "because this warped, murdering traitor wanted a bigger house and a Jaguar."

Aldrich Ames told an interviewer that he believed the spy business itself was based on questionable values and deception. He had simply decided to make money from what he thought was a corrupt system. "I don't believe I was affecting the security of this country," he told reporters.

Ames was fully aware, however, that what he was doing was wrong. While he committed his treason, he had quieted his conscience by refusing to think about the consequences of his actions. "File and forget," Ames often said to himself.

Regardless of his claim that his betrayal of secrets did not affect U.S. security, Ames could not deny that his treason had destroyed the lives of many CIA operatives and their families. When interviewers asked how he could live with that fact, Ames replied, lamely, that in the end he had done as much damage to himself and to his family as to others. "The men I sold . . . . What happened to them happened to me also."

Aldrich Ames will have plenty of time to ponder the consequences of his actions. On April 28, 1994, a U.S. court found him guilty of espionage and sentenced him to life in prison.

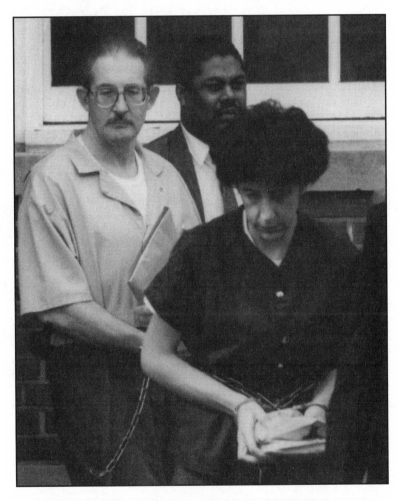

Aldrich Ames and his wife, Rosario, are led from their hearings in a federal courthouse. Rosario was sentenced to 63 months in prison.

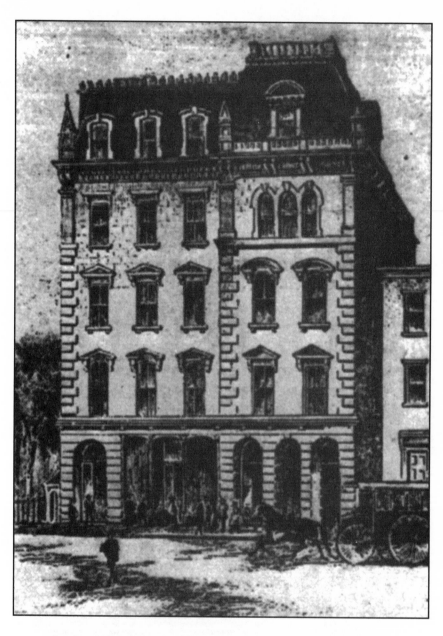

In the 1880s, this building became the first home of the Department of Justice, whose law-enforcement division, the Federal Bureau of Investigation, is responsible for rooting out traitors and spies in the United States.

Bibliography

Ames, Aldrich. "Why I Spied." *New York Times Magazine*, July 31, 1994.

Arbetman, Lee, and Richard Roe, eds. *Great Trials in American History*. St. Paul: West Publishing, 1985.

Barron, John. *Breaking the Ring: The Bizarre Case of the Walker Family Spy Ring*. Boston: Houghton Mifflin, 1987.

Blum, Howard. *I Pledge Allegiance . . . The True Story of the Walkers: An American Spy Family*. New York: Simon & Schuster, 1987.

Boyer, Richard O. *The Legend of John Brown: A Biography and a History*. New York: Knopf, 1973.

Brandt, Clare. *The Man in the Mirror: A Life of Benedict Arnold*. New York: Random House, 1994.

Cohen, Jacob. "The Rosenberg File." *National Review*, July 19, 1993.

"Deadly Mole." *Newsweek*, March 7, 1994.

Draper, Roger. "A Tragedy Without a Hero." *New Republic*, November 8, 1993.

Duffy, Brian. "The Cold War's Last Spy." *U.S. News & World Report*, March 6, 1995.

Duus, Masayo. *Tokyo Rose: Orphan of the Pacific*. New York: Harper and Row, 1979.

Early, Pete. *Family of Spies.* New York: Bantam, 1988.

Fritz, Jean. *Traitor: The Case of Benedict Arnold.* New York: Putnam, 1981.

Hiss, Tony. "My Father's Honor." *New Yorker,* November 16, 1992.

Howard, Edward Lee. *Safe House: The Compelling Story of the Only CIA Operative to Seek Asylum in Russia.* Bethesda, Md.: Nation Press, 1995.

Howe, Russell Warren. *The Hunt for "Tokyo Rose."* Lanham, Md.: Madison Books, 1990.

Leggett, John. "Tokyo Rose: Traitor or Scapegoat?" *New York Times Magazine,* December 5, 1976.

Maas, Peter. *Killer Spy.* New York: Warner Books, 1995.

McGlone, Robert E. "Rescripting a Troubled Past: John Brown's Family and the Harpers Ferry Conspiracy." *Journal of American History,* March 1989.

"Mildred Gillars." *New York Times Biographical Service,* July 1968.

Nizer, Louis. *The Implosion Conspiracy.* New York: Doubleday, 1973.

Oates, Stephen B. *To Purge This Land with Blood.* Amherst: University of Massachusetts Press, 1970, 1984.

Philipson, Ilene. *Ethel Rosenberg: Beyond the Myths.* New York: Franklin Watts, 1988.

Pincher, Chapman. *Traitors: The Anatomy of Treason*. New York: St. Martin's Press, 1987.

Radosh, Ronald, and Joyce Milton. *The Rosenberg File: A Search for the Truth*. New York: Holt, Rinehart and Winston, 1983.

Randall, Willard Sterne. *Benedict Arnold: Patriot and Traitor*. New York: William Morrow, 1990.

Rubenstein, Richard E., ed. *Great Courtroom Battles*. Chicago: Playboy Press, 1973.

"Sally and Rose." *Time*, August 30, 1948.

Scott, John A., and Robert A. Scott. *John Brown of Harper's Ferry*. New York: Facts on File, 1988.

Scott, Otto J. *The Secret Six: John Brown and the Abolitionist Movement*. New York: Times Books, 1979.

Smith, John Chabot. *Alger Hiss: The True Story*. New York: Holt, Rinehart and Winston, 1976.

Smolowe, Jill. "Double Agent." *Time*, March 7, 1994.

Tanenhaus, Sam. "Hiss: Guilty as Charged." *Commentary*, April 1993.

———. *Whittaker Chambers: A Biography*. New York: Random House, 1997.

———. "Witness for the Truth." *National Review*, February 15, 1993.

"Tokyo Rose." *Time*, September 17, 1945.

U.S. Department of Justice. Federal Bureau of
   Investigation. *The Atom Spy Case*. Washington,
   D.C., March 13, 1961 (rev. July 1994).

Walker, Barbara, and Lesley Jane Nonkin. "My
   Husband Was a Spy." *Redbook*, October 1988.

Weiner, Tim, David Johnston, and Neil A. Lewis.
   Betrayal: The Story of Aldrich Ames, an American Spy.
   New York: Random House, 1995.

Wise, David. "The Ames Spy Hunt." *Time*, May 22, 1995.

———. *The Spy Who Got Away*. New York: Random
   House, 1988.

Index

157

158

95, 97, 100-101, 102, 103;
Walker as agent of, 106, 111,
112, 114, 116, 117-118, 119-
121. *See also* Russia
Stalin, Josef, 9, 55, 62, 95
State Department, 55, 60, 61, 64
statute of limitations, 54, 60
Stuart, J. E. B., 48, 51
Sumner, Charles, 42, 43

Thompson, Henry, 42
Time, 56, 64
Toguri, Fumi Iimuro (mother),
75
Toguri, Iva, 10; considered to be
Tokyo Rose, 68, 73, 74, 80-81,
82, 83, 84; early years of, 73,
75; imprisonment of, 80-81;
as Japanese American, 75, 76-
77; loyalty of, to U.S., 77, 80,
85; sentence of, 83, 84; trial
of, 82-83; work of, for Radio
Tokyo, 77-79, 80, 82, 83. *See
also* Tokyo Rose
Toguri, Jun (father), 73, 75
Tokyo Rose, 67, 68, 73, 74, 79,
80, 81, 82, 83, 84. *See also*
Toguri, Iva
Tolkachev, Adolf, 132, 133
Tories, 15, 26, 28, 32
treason: laws concerning, 9-10,
93; nature of, 6, 7-9, 10-11, 93
Truman, Harry S., 56, 81
Turner, Stansfield, 132

United Nations, 56

Vertefeuille, Jeanne, 141
Vietnam War, 9, 114, 121
Volkogonov, Dmitri, 64
Vulture (British ship), 28, 30

Walker, Arthur (brother), 110,
114, 118, 119
Walker, Barbara Crowley

(wife), 107, 108, 110, 111,
113, 114-115, 116, 119, 120
Walker, Cynthia (daughter), 120
Walker, John (Jack), 10; early
years of, 108-109; financial
problems of, 107, 111, 113;
guilty plea of, 119-120;
Navy codes revealed by, 111-
112, 114, 121; sentence of,
120; as Soviet agent, 106,
108, 112-116, 117-118, 119-
121, 148; in U.S. Navy, 106,
107, 110, 111, 112, 113-114,
116
Walker, John, Sr. (father), 108,
109
Walker, Laura (daughter), 116
Walker, Michael (son), 115,
116, 118, 119, 120
Walker, Peggy (mother), 108
War Department, 81
War Information, U.S. Office
of, 71, 81
Washington, George, 19, 24,
25, 27, 28, 29-30, 33
Webster, William, 130, 142
West Point, 28, 29
Whitworth, Jerry, 113, 116,
118, 119, 120
Winchell, Walter, 81, 82
Woolsey, James, 148
World War II, 55, 56, 66, 85, 97,
101; propaganda during, 67-
68, 69, 70, 71, 72, 77-79, 83

Yalta, meeting at, 55
Young Communist League, 89,
90
Yurchenko, Vitaly, 127-128,
132, 133, 140

"Zero Hour," 78, 80, 83

159

ABOUT THE AUTHOR

NATHAN AASENG is an award-winning author of over 100 fiction and nonfiction books for young readers. He writes on subjects ranging from science and technology to business, government and politics to law. Aaseng's books for The Oliver Press include *Great Justices of the Supreme Court*, *America's Third-Party Presidential Candidates*, *Genetics: Unlocking the Secrets of Life*, *You Are the Supreme Court Justice*, *You Are the President*, *You Are the President II*, *You Are the General*, *You Are the General II*, *You Are the Senator*, *You Are the Corporate Executive*, and *You Are the Juror*.

Photo Credits

Photographs courtesy of: cover (bottom right), Reuters/ HO-FBI/ Archive Photos; p. 6, Minnesota Historical Society; pp. 8, 10, 11, 12, 17, 18, 20, 22, 23, 26, 29, 30, 34, 36, 38, 43, 45, 46, 49, 50, 57, 58, 62, 66, 74, 76, 78, 82, 84, 85, 86, 93, 96, 98, 101, 102, 104, Library of Congress; p. 41, Kansas Collection, University of Kansas Libraries; pp. 51, 52, 71, 79, 94, 100, 105, National Archives; p. 55, Novosti Photo; p. 65, Richard Nixon Library; p. 69, Archives of the Simon Wiesenthal Center; pp. 91, 130, 146, 150, Federal Bureau of Investigation; p. 106, U.S. Naval Institute/ Naval Institute Press; p. 109, Lackawanna Historical Society; p. 112, Revilo Pictures; p. 115, D. E. Turner, National Museum of Naval Aviation; pp. 118, 119 (both), 120, 128, 133, UPI/ Corbiss-Bettmann; p. 122, AP/ Wide World Photos; pp. 125, 139, 142, Central Intelligence Agency; p. 134, Reuters/ Ira Schwartz/ Archive Photos; p. 137, University of Wisconsin-River Falls; p. 145, U.S. Department of Justice; p. 149, Reuters/ Karen Anderson/ Archive Photos.

920
AAS

Aaseng, Nathan.

Treacherous
traitors.

DATE			
MR 05 '01	NOV 2		
MR 26 '01	NOV 02		
FE 04 '04			
NOV 19	APR 29		
APR 29			
MAY 13			
MAY 14			
DEC 13			
3/2011			

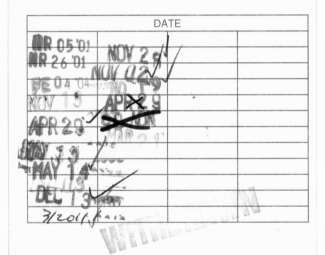

005238   5074975